A Fruitful Harvest.

Essays after Bion

A Fruitful Harvest:

Essays after Bion

Jeffrey L. Eaton

The Alliance Press, Seattle

Published by the Alliance Press, P.O. Box 33762, Seattle, WA 98133. The Alliance Press is the publishing arm of the Northwest Alliance for Psychoanalytic Study. The goal of the Alliance is to make psychoanalytic knowledge available and useful to interested professionals and to the community at large in the Pacific Northwest.

Designed by Dennis Martin

Editorial review by Sigrid Asmus

Printed in the United States of America

ISBN 978-0-9833178-0-7

The author would like to acknowledge that chapter 2 was first published in the *Journal of Melanie Klein and Object Relations*, vol. 16(1), March 1998.

"The Obstructive Object," a paper that originally appeared in *The Psychoanalytic Review*, vol. 92(3) (June 2005): 355–72, is reprinted in chapter 3 with the permission of the National Psychological Association for Psychoanalysis.

The text for chapter 5 first appeared as a chapter in *Into the Mountain Stream: Psychotherapy and Buddhist Experience*, edited by Paul C. Cooper (Lanham, MD: Jason Aronson, 2007), and included a section titled Attention and Pain that is now incorporated in chapter 1.

Photographer credits: Front cover: Pieter Brueghel the Elder, *The Harvesters* (1565), 119 x 162 cm, collection Metropolitan Museum of Art, New York City, courtesy Wikipedia; back cover photograph by K. Mesirow, 2010.

For Myrna and George,

and, especially, for Kay

The analyst must dream what destroys the patient's dreams, and since the analyst may or may not be much better at this than the patient, the analysis turns on two people becoming partners in evolution, doing work that all humanity must come to do. In other words, part of the long-term work involves becoming real to ourselves and to each other and the profound ethics this implies.

— Michael Eigen, *The Sensitive Self* (2004)

Contents

Preface

THE ALLIANCE PRESS, A PROJECT OF THE NORTHWEST Alliance for Psychoanalytic Study, enthusiastically offers this volume of essays by Jeffrey Eaton, MA, FIPA. *A Fruitful Harvest: Essays after Bion* is the author's first published volume as well as the second book the Alliance Press has presented by a unique, leading member of our community.

For many years, Eaton has steadily contributed to the Seattle community through teaching and presenting at our local psychoanalytic training institutes, as well as the COR Northwest Family Development Center (Center for Object Relations) and the Northwest Alliance for Psychoanalytic Study. He has a keen interest in the foundations and implications of the models upon which our psychoanalytic theories are based, and he has a masterful capacity to clarify them and to distinguish them from one another. By virtue of this facility, Eaton engenders lively conversations with representatives of different psychoanalytic perspectives.

Deeply compassionate and dedicated to providing service to those in need, Eaton cofounded the Alliance Community Psychotherapy Clinic, which offers reduced-fee psychotherapy to low-income patients and mentorship and supervision to therapists new to the field. He co-developed, helped to administer, and taught in the clinic's Postgraduate Internship Program. Through all these activities, in addition to a thriving practice of psychoanalysis, psychotherapy, and supervision, Eaton continues to pursue growth as a clinician and a writer. This dedication to growth and his generosity in sharing his thoughts with this community make him an ideal author to bring to a larger audience through this book.

A Fruitful Harvest chronicles significant aspects of Eaton's evolving perspective. He seems to have had an intuitive sense of the questions that were going to help him grow, almost as though compelled to a path that chose him as much as he chose it. His particular interest in the theories of Melanie Klein, Donald Meltzer, Frances Tustin, and especially Wilfred Bion, along with his treatment of autism and belief in the psychic reality of autistic children, have guided his choice of mentors: Michael Eigen, James Gooch, James Grotstein, and Franco Scabbiolo. These psychoanalysts help him engage emergent questions in his search for clinical understanding. While delving into these psychoanalytic pursuits, Eaton began to study and practice Buddhist meditation with guidance from Lama Yeshe Wangmo and the inspiration of her teacher Lama Tharchin Rinpoche. This undertaking has had a deep impact on his sensibility, quietly infuses his clinical practice, and is manifest in this volume of writing. It can be observed in his humane presence, which is at once grounded, welcoming, and compassionate, and it underpins his listening presence with an awake attention and an open and curious mind.

Eaton's clinical work and thinking have been recognized in a variety of ways. Several of the essays in this volume have been previously published in professional journals or edited volumes of collected essays of both psychoanalytic and Buddhist interest. Eaton received the International Frances Tustin Memorial Prize and Lectureship in 2006. He regularly contributes to the Emerging British Object Relations Conference and the Alliance's annual Forum Conference in Seattle and has been invited to lecture in several cities, including Bozeman, Los Angeles, San Francisco, and Berlin. As a member of the International Seminar on Psychoanalytic Intervention and Research on Autism (INSPIRA), he participates in international conferences on autism in New York City, Rome, and London.

The author's writing style is precise and inviting, open and integrative for the reader. He is lucid and capable of making difficult theory transparent and organized. In his writing one can feel in touch with something not easily graspable in the internal workings of being human. Perhaps his remarkable capacity to think and organize finds its most distinctive form in his passionate and diligent pursuit of the theory of Wilfred Bion. *A Fruitful Harvest: Essays after Bion* has something fresh and stimulating to offer both the experienced and the inexperienced readers of Bion.

We on the Northwest Alliance for Psychoanalytic Study's Publications Committee have found Eaton's development remarkable and are aware that his gifts will continue to evolve; to use the metaphor of his title, while this book is a fruitful harvest, it is also a packet of seeds. As the author says, these essays are yet to be cultivated into a full field: he offers something well thought out while also leaving space for more to grow. We hope that reading this book will stimulate new ideas to be integrated into clinical application and will kindle more questions for further exploration.

— *The editors of the Alliance Press: Jeanne Castle and Kris Wheeler, cochairs; Joan Dinkelspiel, Ginger Harstad Glawe, Kathy Knowlton, Helen Palisin, Carol Poole, and Marcia Robbins*

Acknowledgments

I HAVE FOND MEMORIES OF MY GRANDMOTHER, IRENE Brown, and of Lena McCammon, who was like a grandmother to me. I imagine they each would have enjoyed seeing this book.

Paul Ingendaay and Scott L. Montgomery provided vivid early examples of men working persistently, intelligently, and passionately toward expressing their own unique views as writers. Their friendships were formative and gave me a lasting sense of the intellectual adventure of becoming a writer.

Professionally, I have learned from many friends, colleagues, and mentors. I have benefited immeasurably from nearly twenty years of friendship and conversation with Morry Tolmach, who continues to share his wisdom and zest for life. Terry Hanson and Tom Saunders taught me much over years of conversation. Austin Case was a generative figure in my contact with the reality of primitive mental states.

I have gained much confidence from learning with teachers like Elie Debbané, Stanley Mandell, Ivri Kumin, Stephen Rush, Oscar Romero, Maxine Anderson, and Marianne Robinson. Franco Scabbiolo has been an especially significant mentor over many years, and I deeply appreciate his generosity in sharing both his own and Donald Meltzer's views, particularly in relation to child treatment and the importance of dream life. James Gooch provided an intimate introduction to Bion's work and also deepened my capacity for contact with psychic reality in my clinical work. I am very grateful to Jim Grotstein for agreeing to write the foreword for this collection as well as to Michael Eigen for his many communications. Both men are especially inspiring figures who have provided much valued encouragement over the years. I return to their writings repeatedly for inspiration and for further insights into a lively, evolving version of psychoanalysis. I also bow to Lama Yeshe Wangmo, who has freely shared her deep and authentic experience of Tibetan Buddhism in many intimate conversations. She is a special source of inspiration.

Among the many people who have played a part in helping me to develop my ideas, I have enjoyed numerous creative conversations with Enid Young and Norma Tracey. Ellen Pearlman and Marlene Goldsmith have encouraged my writing through years of Internet conversation. I'm especially grateful to the members of my Bion study group who give me a lively place to learn and to try out new ideas in a creative atmosphere. Judith and Ted Mitrani have been consistently supportive in addition to opening new doors for me. I also thank the Frances Tustin Memorial Trust for the opportunity to present versions of chapters 4 and 8 for the Frances Tustin Memorial Prize Lectures. Paul Cooper welcomed my work and published one of the essays reprinted here. Paul has generously shared his views of Buddhism and psychoanalysis in many e-mail discussions. The Evolving British Object Relations conference in Seattle gave me the occasion to present chapters 6 and 7. The Forum conferences held by the Northwest Alliance for Psychoanalytic Study provided opportunities to present versions of chapters 1 and 9. I have also presented some of this material at the Northern Rockies Psychoanalytic Institute in Bozeman, Montana. I have come to sincerely value these opportunities to share my work with interested colleagues.

I continue to grow by contact with many people in the Northwest Family Development Center / Center for Object Relations, the Northwest Center for Psychoanalysis–Seattle, the Seattle Psychoanalytic Society and Institute, and the Psychoanalytic Center of California. I give special thanks to my teachers and colleagues at Northwestern Psychoanalytic Society in Seattle for sustaining a place where Klein's work and the work of British Object Relations can be studied, discussed, and developed.

The Alliance has been an important organization in my professional development. Over several years, the interns at the Alliance Community Psychotherapy Clinic encouraged me to risk greater self-expression as an instructor. Kris Wheeler and Ginger Harstad Glawe encouraged my writing, and this book is the result, in part, of their spirited support.

Jeanne Castle shepherded the project to publication with consistent enthusiasm. Sigrid Asmus provided valuable advice as well as expert editorial skill. I thank Dennis Martin for his excellent design and production work. I acknowledge the members of the Alliance Publication Committee, especially Joan Dinkelspiel, Ginger Harstad Glawe, Kathy Knowlton, Helen Palisin, Carol Poole, and Marcia Robbins, who each gave valuable time to read and comment on the final manuscript. Finally, I'm especially grateful to the board of the Alliance for publishing this collection as part of their mission to support psychoanalytic thinking in the Pacific Northwest.

I would have little to say without the challenging and continuously evolving work with each of my patients who I am grateful to for allowing me to participate in their transformations. The clinical material in these essays reflects an intimate personal process that exceeds adequate description. Out of respect for confidentiality all names have been changed, and in some instances material has been altered or disguised. I likewise acknowledge with gratitude the many clinicians who I have had the opportunity and privilege to work with as a consultant.

I dedicate this book to my parents, George and Myrna. Their fortitude and love remain deeply important to me. I am especially grateful to my wife, Kay. Without her love and encouragement I would not be the person I enjoy becoming. She is a sincere example of the benefits of encountering and being able to live with "a good heart."

Seattle, Washington
December 2010

Foreword

James S. Grotstein

JEFFREY EATON WRITES IN A MOST ENGAGING WAY. HIS chapters are essays rather than formal scientific presentations, which is his way of presenting a "fruitful harvest" of his experiences—both to himself and to us, the readers, who are allowed, as it were, to look over his shoulder. In this first collection of his writing, it is as if he has just come in from the field where he has been toiling with the anguish of others and his own anguish in response and can now at last *reflect* upon what he has experienced—as well as share his reflections with us. Put another way, this wondrous collection of seamlessly connected essays constitutes a rich and engaging personal diary of the author's efforts in his work and his meditations about what he has found. In the directness of his writing style, one nevertheless comes to recognize a pragmatic, down-to-earth, highly credible and applicable mysticism. The stars on his compass include Wilfred Bion, Michael Eigen, Donald Meltzer, Frances Tustin, and Donald Winnicott, to mention only a few.

A sentence in the introduction epitomizes his central concerns: "My hope for this volume is that it may bring together evidence of two central qualities of mind that I am striving to realize: intelligence and heart." After reading this work, my verdict is that he has richly accomplished his goal. Perhaps one may summarize his recommendations with his own words: "The analytic experience encourages us to wrestle with our fears and to gradually welcome suffering more fully into the moment.... Over time we grow more tolerance for anxieties that would not have been registered or welcomed earlier. We discover how factors like attention, anxiety, and desire shape perception."

The poignancy of what he has brought us from his work is due in no small measure to his caseload. He works with children as well as adults and is very sensitive to outpourings of the most infantile depths of his child and adult patients. His clinical experience in working analytically with autistic and Asperger patients puts him in a rarified realm of experience. Many of the patients who have come to him would be considered untreatable by most other therapists, who often lack both his particular background training in the treatment of primitive mental states of this kind, as well as his patience, his faith, his humility, and the obvious caretaking love he so readily provides for his patients.

An all too brief summary of Eaton's theme would be as follows: He, as an analyst, is poised both to observe and to experience his patients' mental pain, pain that has originated in the impact of their earlier emotional experiences. Pain of this kind worsens if the patient refuses to accept it, that is, to bear it and try to understand it rather than just *endure* or attempt to evade it. It lessens if the patient accepts, and can come to *suffer* it and seeks to understand or objectify it. In order for a patient to be able to successfully suffer her or his emotionally painful experiences, the person, child or adult, must be natively able to tolerate frustration, and especially the frustration of waiting, which in turn is made possible by having faith that helpful answers or objects with answers will arrive soon enough to temper the distress. Some patients may not be able to find the faith that begets frustration tolerance because of having a natively (primary) challenged mind (as in autism or Asperger's syndrome); others may be unable to do so as a result of having experienced an infantile catastrophe due to various traumata. In either case the analyst must initially serve as the patient's auxiliary mind, providing basic functions in much the way a respirator is emergently required for highly distressed patients with serious physical illnesses.

Among the leading themes that the author highlights, in addition to the psychoanalytic study of pain, are the pernicious importance of envy in the clinical situation, the problem of the projective identification rejecting object, the complexity of the essential quality of the analyst's focused attention on the patient, the benefits he has obtained from his immersion in Buddhism and meditation, and the investigation of dreams, both his own and those of his patients. All of this can be summarized, in addition to the theme of listening, as amounting to an exploration of the analyst's professional use of personal experience and as a penetrating attempt to describe how one uses the self in the analytic process.

This book represents an important introduction to Jeffrey Eaton's thought and allows us to welcome the harvest he has gathered from his many years as a therapist working steadily and effectively on the frontier of difficult-to-treat illnesses. We are grateful to him for this highly informative, helpful, and sincere personal testimony of his experiences.

James S. Grotstein, MD, is clinical professor of psychiatry at the David Geffen School of Medicine, UCLA, and training and supervising analyst at the New Center for Psychoanalysis and the Psychoanalytic Center of California, Los Angeles.

Introduction

PSYCHOANALYSIS MEANS MANY THINGS TO MANY different people. The psychoanalyst who has had and continues to have the greatest impact on me is the English writer and theorist W. R. Bion. These essays reflect my sense of the continuing force of his work and my evolving engagement with it and record the traces of accruing awareness. While they clearly reflect influences from others, Bion's inspiration pervades every chapter. Here, I share some of the things that psychoanalysis means to me *after* Bion.

As a writer, I value everyday language. I write both to think and to communicate. I prefer the essay as a form because it is more open than a "scientific" paper. An essay may often be only the entrance to a much deeper set of questions. The essay allows for the personal voice and for exploration of a subject from many different points of view. The essays here link a number of themes and are, inevitably, incomplete. I view these essays as moments in description, stepping stones toward a richer understanding. My hope for this volume is that it may bring together evidence of two central qualities of mind that I am striving to realize: intelligence and heart.

As a psychoanalyst, I work with children and adults, and this experience defines the place from which I speak. There is nothing strange or esoteric about what I do: for five days a week people come to my office and I listen to them. Through participating in the psychoanalytic process, I learn about what makes people suffer and develop.

It is easy to feel that there is too much pain all around us. Often, the intensity of pain can make it feel too intimidating to look at or to listen to. It is natural to recoil from suffering, both in others and in ourselves. I believe that taking the time to learn about another person's experience is a valuable activity all on its own. Psychoanalysis sponsors what I have called an improbable conversation—not because of the content of what is explored, but because of the generous time and expansive attention given by both partners to investigating the complexity and impact of everyday experience.

The psychoanalytic method creates a space in which to investigate the troubling and intimate details of ordinary emotions in people's lives. We need others to help us comprehend our experiences. As I understand it, the psychoanalytic process opens possibilities and conditions in which the participants may explore suffering, come to identify its causes and conditions, and find ways to overcome some of the unconscious habits that perpetuate suffering.

The analytic experience encourages us to wrestle with our fears, and gradually to welcome suffering more fully into the moment. The experience of deepening awareness attunes us to registers not ordinarily listened for or experienced. Over time we grow more tolerance for anxieties that would not have been registered or welcomed earlier. We discover how factors like attention, anxiety, and desire shape perception. We learn to dip into a space for suffering, to stay a little longer, and to emerge again. All this hard work strengthens the self, expands consciousness, and promotes creative problem solving and honest self expression.

Another important approach to suffering comes from meditation. Over the years I have developed a deepening interest in Buddhist psychology. Psychoanalysis and Buddhism share the concern for how mind and body interact to give rise to subjectivity and consciousness. Part of the exploration of ordinary suffering involves realizing how alienated we can be from the complex interweaving of layers of mind and body experience. Both psychoanalysis and meditation can be entrances to an embodied psychology, to learning about the way consciousness is grounded in bodily emotional life. Far from being "all in your head," psychoanalysis and Buddhism can each sponsor ways of becoming familiar with the energies and impulses of embodied psychic life.

A key path to deepening awareness is the investigation of attention. For me, most days begin with meditation practice. I sit and watch my thoughts, notice my breath, and relax my body. I become aware of sensations, impulses, images, feelings, memories, wishes, and stories. Through meditation I have learned how active the mind always is and how many things go on simultaneously at the border of consciousness. Over time, I have learned how to rest my mind, using techniques like focusing attention on the sound of a mantra as I chant. Often I feel a deepening sense of presence as I relax. Instead of spacing out, paradoxically, meditation sponsors a feeling of vivid presence.

Another important practice is self-analysis through dream investigation. For many years I have recorded my dreams, and I have a practice of observing and describing the emotions and images of my dream life. Staying in touch with dream life is a way of taking the pulse of the imagination.

Psychoanalysis and Buddhism both have things to say about how to get to know ourselves and the world. They both help us, as Wallace Stevens said somewhere, "to walk barefoot in reality." The combination of being in analysis and of learning meditation can provide a way to allow each process simultaneously to support the other, on parallel tracks, and help to set in place and strengthen a floor for deepening emotional experience. These two traditions are like tributaries flowing into the larger stream of life becoming aware of itself.

Freud noted a century ago how important it is to keep finding ways to contact reality. Psychoanalysis and Buddhism deeply question our constructions of reality and reveal how concrete our beliefs can become, how unquestioned our assumptions often are. Whatever reality is, it always exceeds our ability to comprehend and to describe it. Both the practice of psychoanalysis and that of Buddhism offer vehicles for exploring reality from a deeply personal point of view—from the inside out. Inspired by both traditions, I keep trying to widen my contact with reality and to expand and deepen my experience of it. Gradually, I have begun to develop faith that by facing suffering and speaking honestly about it we can gather some personal wisdom and share it together.

Investigating suffering, surprisingly, can reconnect us to a freshness that is at once natural and vitalizing and one of the deepest aspects of reality. It's not something created, it simply exists to be recognized as we come through suffering into deeper awareness. Both psychoanalysis and Buddhism can help us to clear away the obstacles that obstruct the awareness of this natural freshness and creativity. When we can meet pain with compassion we can drop some of our identifications with suffering, and the sensation of this natural openness can be acknowledged and trusted even during very difficult times.

These essays reflect my attempts to make personal both psychoanalytic and Buddhist training and encompass nearly twenty years of clinical experience and meditation practice. From this fruitful harvest, I seek to become more confident and attentive (more skillful, I hope) at looking, feeling, observing, imagining, intuiting, communicating, and expanding my ability to contact and share the present moment.

In chapter 1 I describe the central problem for every treatment, and what I call "the fate of pain." Chapter 2 investigates the work of Bion and others on destructiveness through the eyes of the influential contemporary analyst Michael Eigen. In chapter 3 I explore a key idea found in Bion's work: the influence of a projective identification rejecting object that Bion called "an obstructive object." According to Bion, the obstructive object becomes an internal ego-destructive factor significant in many forms of mental pain. Chapter 4 tells the story of the treatment of a young autistic boy whom I call Eric. I also describe the importance of Frances Tustin's pioneering work in the treatment of autism. Chapter 5 makes links between Buddhist practice and psychotherapy as well as offering personal descriptions of the impact of learning to meditate. Here I link such themes as emotion, attention, and mental pain with what I call "nowhere" states of mind. Chapter 6 reflects on the significance of dreaming in Donald Meltzer's work, and chapter 7 briefly tackles various meanings of envy in the Kleinian and post-Kleinian traditions. Chapters 8 and 9 can be viewed as companion essays that explore the important theme of "deepening reverie"; chapter 8 introduces the function of "attention" in psychoanalysis, and the concluding chapter explores the idea of "listening to yourself listening to another."

■   ■   ■

The poet, essayist, and farmer Wendell Berry has spoken about how it is impossible to give advice about or to meaningfully characterize something called "American farming." Indeed, Berry opines that one cannot even speak of farming in Kentucky, or in Harlan County, where he has lived for decades. Instead, according to Berry, one's authority derives from the embodied memory of tending one's own chunk of earth over many years. We live in the present, but we draw upon the experience of the past as we make the present conscious. My own sense is that farming is not the only area where caring for one's work expands the field of meaning.

The essays collected here are the seeds of future harvests too. I see the future outlines of my work as a psychoanalyst, tending my own clinical garden, contained in the subjects that compel my attention: autism, listening, dreaming and symbol formation, and the problems of destructiveness and violence. Each of these areas may someday blossom as a book of its own.

But it is the process of clearing, plowing, planting, and harvesting that is the real work, and in its own way that work is a modest and sustainable source of ordinary beauty, joy, and even, hopefully, wisdom.

A Fruitful Harvest

Essays after Bion

CHAPTER 1

The Fate of Pain

THE BASIC QUESTION IN EVERY TREATMENT IS THIS: What is the fate of pain? The details of how an individual copes with pain, whether physical or emotional, become an essential area of investigation. Intense emotional pain gives rise to numerous conscious and unconscious strategies that all have in common the goal of removing pain from awareness. One can fight pain, deny it, go numb to it, rage against it, dissociate from it, or mask it (temporarily) with substances like alcohol, cocaine, or heroin. In extreme states, such as schizophrenia, the English psychoanalyst Wilfred Bion theorized that one can attack and dismantle the ego and its modes of perception in order not to register pain. All these strategies, obviously, tend to increase pain in the long run rather than lessening it.

In this culture there is a deep sense of personal isolation and social alienation that arises, at least in part, from our failure to skillfully relate to pain. We are not trained to deal mindfully with pain. But because experiencing pain in many forms is an inevitable part of being alive in the world, we need methods for relating to, thinking about, and working with pain.

When too much pain comes too fast or too early (we are never really prepared for pain), our minds and bodies can feel overwhelmed and then we automatically begin to shut down. The experience of shock impacts both mind and body. As shock fades, pain tends to capture our attention. We can feel hostage to the sensations of pain. Thresholds of tolerance vary in both physical and mental pain. Our fear is that pain will grow bigger and bigger until it is equated with the whole of reality. The terror of a feeling that there is no escape adds to the fear of pain. It is the intensity of fear that generates a hatred of pain.

Bion speaks of the psychotic state as one characterized by a hatred of reality. What the psychotic person hates is unmodulated pain—that is, pain unmediated by compassion, respect, and understanding. Bion described how the excessive use of projective identification to remove pain from awareness becomes entrenched as a style of coping in the psychotic part of the personality. In the most severe cases, the mind becomes a kind of machine for evacuation. Thoughts and feelings are treated like bizarre or toxic things to be destroyed. No space for registering pain or frustration is allowed to develop. From Bion's point of view, these conditions may permanently obstruct the development of thinking, feeling, and experiencing.

Psychotherapy counters such tendencies by bringing attention to the way we process or fail to face pain. In psychotherapy, pain is investigated interpersonally. We strive to find an emotional language to describe and transform the experience of pain. As analysts we hope to free people from both subjective and actual isolation and to help them stop hiding from and hating their pain. In the analytic dialogue, attention is focused on the phenomenology of thinking and feeling and how pain intrudes upon or stimulates the capacity to use the mind and body creatively.

Observing Pain

It sounds counterintuitive to recommend learning to observe pain. Won't focusing on the experience of pain make it worse? Actually, just the opposite is often true. Pain becomes unbearable to the degree that we actively fight against it. Denial of pain creates impasse. Hatred of the often shameful feelings that seem to arise around painful experience only compounds the sense of helplessness and fear. Psychotherapy sometimes makes possible the special conditions necessary to begin to observe pain and to gradually transform the experience of it by tolerating and describing it.

We are too often deeply ignorant of the actual details of our own experiences of pain. We have never learned to "soften" to pain in order to create the mental space necessary to closely observe it. Opening to pain helps a person to discover and to expand tolerance. Shinzen Young, a meditation teacher, offers this formula: suffering = pain x resistance to pain. If we can lessen our resistance to pain, we can learn, for example, how to observe how much judgment and fear we unconsciously project into our pain. The benefits of becoming familiar with our ways of coping with pain are immediately tangible.

When we limit our judgments about pain, when we soften to it, we can come to know from experience that pain is not monolithic. It has many textures and shifting qualities. Pain is not permanent, though our fear of pain may make it seem so. When fear is unmodified it tends to create a momentum that manifests as hatred. More than pain itself, we are often afraid of unknown intensities and the untested limits of what we might bear. When desperately pained, the images that arise from our fears become objects, concretized and insistent. A kind of negative feedback loop gets going. When we find that we can face our fears, a sense of confidence and acceptance begins to grow naturally. It is not about being in control; rather, observing pain helps to cultivate a state of mind that might simply be called the capacity to be present.

Processing Pain

When working with patients, it is very important to offer sincere empathy for their experiences. Our task is to get to know the particulars of how each person does or doesn't process pain successfully. My friend Morry has often encouraged me to ask myself how people picture their emotions. He has taught me to ask myself several questions while listening to a patient: What does anxiety look like? What does it feel like? What does it taste like, smell like, and sound like? These kinds of questions can be applied to any emotional experience. They are a way of imaginatively entering the person's experience, of trying to put oneself directly in the other's shoes.

Our descriptions must be embodied, not abstract. Often people need our words in order to help to find their own. Our words need to be direct, sincere, and emotionally accurate, not vague, formulaic, or theoretical. If one is unable to achieve this level of imaginative intimacy with another person's experience, it is very difficult to find words to adequately lend a sense of our presence.

When some patients seek treatment, whether they are children or adults, their progress is ineluctably linked with learning to bear the experience of emotional catastrophe. This is a challenge not only for the patient, but also, and often intensely, for the therapist. Sometimes the impact of another person's suffering can be more than simply heard in their words or felt through their sobs. Suffering can be tangibly seen, viscerally felt, and bloodily tasted in the unfolding analytic moment.

I mean this description neither absolutely literally nor completely poetically. There is a perceptual space in clinical work that is a paradox, an intersection between concreteness and metaphor. Inhabiting such a potential space allows for the possibility of sharing the intensity of a person's emotional storm. The very intensity of this kind of intimate participation calls into question the resiliency of the therapist's attention and separate space for observation. Such intensity strains, but hopefully also grows, the capacity of both the patient and the therapist to bear and transform emotional pain.

I have noticed that many people tend to unconsciously employ a language of catastrophe when speaking of intense emotional pain. They speak of tornadoes, fires, floods, earthquakes, and other shockingly powerful forces. That choice of images must be taken seriously. Many patients have equated unregulated emotional experience with forces too great for human intervention or comprehension.

Patients' descriptions are sometimes so powerfully convincing and so intense that for a number of sessions the therapist can become frightened too. This fear is never just about the patient's emotional experience. Importantly, I become aware of the intensity of my own reactions. The emotional storm emerges in the field between me and the patient.

Working through my own feelings, I sometimes must cope with intense sensations, images, and fears. I have had sessions where I felt as if I would run out of my own consulting room. In such moments I have learned to soften to the awfulness. I once found myself saying to myself "I can't stand this any longer." Another voice came to my rescue and said "You can stand it. You are standing it. What you can't stand are the automatic judgments you are making about your pain without reflecting upon them."

Getting a sense of the gap between unpleasant and painful sensations and the meanings we automatically assign them (like "I can't stand this" or "I hate this" or "I want to die") is a huge step in learning how to work with intense situations. By noticing a gap between the sensation and the unreflective thought assigned to it, we can create a much-needed space for beginning to tolerate experience.

Intense pain tends to intimidate people: the greater the intensity, the greater the intimidation. When you add duration to intensity, the toll on the ego can become very high. Sometimes we feel our way along as if on a tightrope in the dark. Eventually we cross to the other side and find a somewhat wider path. Often it is important to become mindful of each step. It is important not to give in to the feeling of intimidation or helplessness. We learn over time to hold our pain without amplifying it or denying it.

For some patients my task seems to be to draw attention to the inner world so that it comes into clear view and can be appreciated. For others, my task is to modulate and reduce the oppressive intensity of emotional experience by doing my best to hold the pain that is emerging, to lend words when possible, and sincerely to be present as a witness to what no one else may ever have been able to stay with or describe.

The process of transforming pain is, literally, a day-by-day project—sometimes minute by minute, sometimes even breath by breath—accomplished by tolerating it, picturing it, describing it, sharing it, exploring it, dreaming it, and learning to swim in it.

However, I cannot suffer for my patients. I register my own emotional experiences and from that sincere place I follow as closely and as openly as I can. I try to find words in the moment and to offer a special kind of attention. But I have no magic answers or solutions. Part of my pain is that I cannot simply remove the pain my patients must face. In the best cases, we can literally learn to play with pain together.

Over the years of work together people grow a deeper capacity for loving connections, and, perhaps most importantly, some soften into strength and become curious about, even compassionate toward, some of the most pained parts of themselves. The pain is not gone, but one has a very different relationship to it, and to the idea of how others might experience it. △ relationship to pain

Conclusion

Pain is a given. To be human and alive exposes you to the experience of pain. From a psychological point of view, pain is not really the problem. Rather, it is our relationship to pain, and in particular our mental habits and how we do or don't make space for pain, that make all the difference. We can gain a great deal of insight into how to handle pain if we investigate openly how harshly we judge and fight our pain.

The practical task of psychoanalysis is to identify, describe, and over time to transform the unconscious modes of coping with pain that we learned very early in life, modes that can be observed in transferences into the present. Our task is to learn to describe (and in doing so, to contain and bring awareness to) the shifting levels of pain and anxiety that the patient experiences, moment to moment and session to session. Given time, the mindfulness and reverie that we demonstrate for our patients is internalized and becomes part of the patient's own creative capacity and style of relating to experience. (+ to self)

CHAPTER 2

On Psychic Deadness

*Our pains will petrify when our gestures no longer make sense. But our tears ...
who will take them on himself?*

— Edmond Jabès

SINCE THE PUBLICATION OF *THE PSYCHOTIC CORE* IN 1986, Michael Eigen has gradually and with gentle ferocity introduced his audiences to a new species of clinical writing. Is there such a thing as a contemporary psychoanalytic sensibility? Eigen would probably argue against unity in favor of plurality and speak of multiple potential sensibilities. Multiple voices arise from the experience of attending with cultivated awareness to the almost infinitely ripe encounter between self and other. All of Eigen's writings question how we can bear and later make use of this abundance of experience. According to Eigen, "We are all in the business of growing a psyche capable of meeting the tasks that having a psyche generates" (1992, p. xiii).

Over the years, through a number of books, Eigen has introduced his readers to a new clinical lexicon. An "area of faith" arises from the successful experience of "coming through" psychic change and psychic catastrophe. "A distinction–union structure pervades experience" (1992, p. xi). The phenomenology of a psychotic core "can be components of a broad range of emotional states and mental disorders" (1986, p vi). Among his enduring preoccupations is the description of a vital interdependence between self–other relationships and mind–body sensations. "In my experience," Eigen writes, "tuning into what body self and mental self are doing is an indispensable part of useful clinical encounter. In a sense, my work is a kind of biography of body self/mental self in heart-to-heart, mind-to-mind encounter" (1992, p. xv).

Perhaps because of his early and extended work with psychosis, Eigen is particularly sensitive to the emotional *impact* that the patient ineluctably has upon the analyst. This impact is not to be diminished but investigated thoroughly. Opening to the suffering of another soul is almost an ethical imperative in Eigen's brand of analysis. Over and over again he questions and encourages the analyst's capacity for precision, compassion, and mental spaciousness. The eighteen essays that comprise *Psychic Deadness* (1996) amount to a kind of plea for "a new and better movement between aliveness and deadness" (p. xvi).

In *Psychic Deadness*, Eigen revisits some of his favorite concerns and expands them in various directions. Self–other and mind–body phenomena are again close to the center: "In my books and papers I explore aspects of a split between an occultly transcendent mental self and a fusional-explosive body self. This split is the core pathological structure of our time" (p. 103).

Eigen's exploration of this "core pathological structure of our time" includes various meditations on selected aspects of the work of Freud, Klein, Bion, and Winnicott. Though Eigen is inspired by many others (among them Lacan, Jung, Ferenczi, and Milner), it is Bion and Winnicott whose spirits pervade this book. In *The Psychotic Core*, he writes that "The horrific has a beauty of its own, its own ecstasy, and we ought not to walk around it as if it were not there, no more than we should become one with it" (1986, p. viii). The same can now be said for varieties of psychic deadness. Eigen marshals an expansive acuity and attention to minute description inspired by Bion and marries these capacities with an appreciation of paradox and a determination to personalize experience inspired by Winnicott. Most important to Eigen, however, is the honest tracking of an unfolding of his own psychic transformations in which "subject-to-subject impact speaks" (1996, p. xxiii).

When Bion interposed the symbol of the double arrow to represent a to and fro between Klein's paranoid-schizoid and depressive positions, he multiplied the variations that the analyst might observe in the moment-to-moment encounter with the patient. Eigen (1996) builds on this structure and double-arrow dialectics proliferate. Throughout part one, titled "Theoretical Soundings," Eigen helps the reader track phenomena through the use of dialectics that include: mechanical ↔ flow, concrete

↔ intangible, reduction ↔ complexity, too much ↔ too little, assertive ↔ receptive, fullness ↔ emptiness, emotionlessness ↔ anxiety, fantasy ↔ reality, creative ↔ destructive, holding ↔ letting go, creating ↔ nulling, and exploring ↔ foreclosing. Though rarely explicitly referring to Bion's model of container–contained, Eigen has developed and refined his own way of working from Bion's model. In Eigen's hands Bion's container–contained becomes an organizing yet dynamic entry point to the unlimited phenomenological richness of the moment to moment encounter of two minds.

Eigen loves working with primary process. "In an important way, loving the flow of primary process meanings has made my life worthwhile" (1996, p. 142). Eigen speaks of primary process as a "capacity." He urges the reader to "celebrate the linking power of primary process work" (p. 142). This creative capacity is contrasted with a nulling force, a destructive force described by Bion that, as Eigen writes, "goes on working after it destroys existence, time, and space" (p. 35). In a horrific image of a certain kind of psychic deadness, Eigen states, "There is no end to nulling" (p. 35). But in more hopeful situations primary process and pain are intimately partnered. Primary process *works on the pain* (p. 20). According to Eigen,

> Mastery of pain is too much to expect. But perhaps primary process can bite off bits of painful impacts, rework painful injuries in fragmentary ways. Reworking of pain is always partial. One cannot make savage wounds go away. But little by little, primary process can absorb more of the impact, keep turning shock around, make room for the shock. Growth of even a little digestive capacity goes a long way. (p. 21)

The passage above is indicative of much of Eigen's voice throughout *Psychic Deadness*. On one hand, this example is a useful primer on the healing value Freud placed on associative flow, especially in his early work. But there is more here than a retelling of Freud. There is a confidence and a personal quality to Eigen's writing, as if he were sharing a journal entry or a seminar note with the reader. His celebration of flow comes through in his style. He allows for the play of *his* many voices.

Throughout *Psychic Deadness* the reader hears Eigen in a plethora of roles as analyst, as teacher, as supervisor. You also hear him reflect on his own vulnerabilities and uncertainties. He shares his excitement and his doubt. You are invited to participate with a yearning part, a striving part, a seeking part, even a straining-at-song and lamentation part of the author. You catch the poetic and prophetic strands that Eigen allows expression, and you learn that he sometimes worries that such honesty marginalizes his work and limits his audience.

Eigen has spent considerable time digesting some of Bion's more elusive ideas. There are important discussions of Bion's idea of "no-thing." Eigen elaborates the reality of an immoral conscience, mechanisms of psychic murder, and the powerful anti-experience forces that are generated. These chapters are too dense to summarize but a taste, at least, can be offered:

> One can use symbols to represent or get rid of emotional reality. Symbols usable in a process of discovery express gaps susceptible to investigation. Fertile symbols mix the known and unknown in productive ways. They hold the unknown (no-thing) open so that growth is possible. The same image, sound, movement, or letter grouping can be part of an attempt to evacuate and null emotional reality. Perhaps one cannot take the build-up of tension involved in the growth of a thought or feeling. Perhaps life has taught one to hate emotional reality...(1996, p. 55)

In many ways grappling with these hateful and nulling states is crucial to an appreciation of Eigen's larger project of describing how psychotherapy sponsors a process of coming alive as a person, described through almost all his work. Struggling to appreciate the ways that an "anti-representational attitude" is created and solidified enables the reader to sustain a foreground–background dialogue that offers the possibility of being open and alive to the experience of the abundance of psychic flow. Terrible states of blackness, concreteness, and deadness may flood or stick or bring the psyche to a trembling halt. These chapters are both difficult to stay with and to comprehend (they strain the reader), and at the same time they are rewarding and exciting. In this way they mirror the experience of working with such hard-to-reach individuals. This area is crucial clinically, and Eigen's work contributes to sustaining and enlarging the space for thinking about such challenging patients pioneered by Bion, Segal, Rosenfeld, and others.

When Eigen writes of Winnicott there is always a sense of deep appreciation for his accomplishments and generosity of spirit. Eigen uses Winnicott to balance the weightiness of Klein and Bion. It is not that Winnicott did not appreciate madness like Klein or Bion, or that he did not sound the depths in his own way, but for Eigen, Winnicott opens up an explicit and necessary perspective on hope. We must not only grow a psyche capable of sustaining the encounters with hatred, deadness, madness, and joy, but we must also evolve "psychosomatic equipment sufficient to support it" (p. 86). For Winnicott, destructiveness is linked to a primitive kind of love, and Eigen sets this experience, alongside similar experiences described by Freud, Klein, and Bion, to give the reader a multidimensional picture of the kinds of darkness that the psyche must struggle courageously to come through with the sensitive help of the analyst.

Part two of *Psychic Deadness* introduces "Clinical Soundings" and covers a great deal of territory through evocative vignettes drawn from the treatment of several patients. Some analysts feel that there is not enough honest discussion of what it feels like to do this work. We don't really explore together in enough detail the analyst's internal experience and how it is used. Eigen never seems to shy away from frankly spelling out his experience, sometimes in provocative ways. For example, he writes:

> I sank into the pain I felt when she spoke to me, when I looked at her. I sank into the pain of our eye contact, into the bliss and pain of our skin contact. Yes, skin contact, although our bodies never touched. I felt our eye–skin contact was very strong. We sat in chairs across a small room, separated by several feet. I was keenly aware how permeable our skin was. We swam in and out of each other through our skin. (p. 129)

Perhaps this is an example of the analyst's openness to "staying with an experience and letting it build" (p. 92) rather than shutting down to experience, getting rid of it, or relying on a second skin of sophistication to defend against the anxieties of a powerfully compelling sense of subjective merger.

Throughout "Clinical Soundings," Eigen offers bits and pieces of his work, accompanied by extended meditations that branch off sometimes in many directions. The wish for more detailed examples of encounters (what did he really say?) between patient and analyst will be frustrated (but see Eigen 1992 and 1995). Yet reflecting on the fragments offered still proves richly evocative. Eigen suggests new roles for the analyst, such as being an "auxiliary primary processor" or a "true self counterpart." Often the descriptions of his work and his patients' subjectivity are poignant and powerful. He makes novel and creative use of phenomena like "emptiness" and "shock." He seems to consistently take up the *other* side(s) of an issue, continuously expanding and opening new dimensions for his and his patient's consideration. In the chapter "Winning Lies," Eigen even ventures into political and social reflections, an area too little attended to and written about by the analyst-as-citizen.

In one compelling example, Eigen speaks of the analyst's function as a "range finder" (p. 107), tuning in to the patient's psychic state and area of *being*. He also writes of the consequences of not having developed a sensitive enough range finder: "If the therapist directs his remarks to the person when the person has vacated to region after region of nonperson, his efforts are likely to be appropriated by fringes of a dead false self system and shuttled toward the vortex to disappear" (p. 107).

According to Albert Mason (personal communication, 1997), Bion often recommended trying a "sighting shot" as part of making an interpretation. Eigen develops a similar idea in greater detail, suggesting that if the analyst's range finder is accurate enough, the patient will gradually introject and develop a range finder of her own, helping her to learn how to dip in and out of self experiences in a more fluid and natural way. One needs to be able to navigate inside in order to be truly open to being among others.

The final chapter of the book, titled "Boas and Flowers," is especially challenging. Eigen, an analyst who has to a great degree become associated with treating very difficult patients, reflects on a single encounter with a patient who did not stay to engage in treatment. The reflections in this chapter range from Eigen's straining to assess his own limitations to wondering about a new cultural moment when patients *shop* for therapists and test-drive treatments. Nowhere in this book is Eigen more raw than in this chapter as he puts the reader directly into his inner world, describing in swirling detail the reverberations that rang through him during the impact of his brief encounter.

Questioning must be a style of life for Eigen. His interest in the growth-producing as well as the pathological twisting of aspects of the ideal and the mystical are never simpleminded or naive. Throughout his writings we find clear statements of the value and complexity of opening to contact with the unspeakable and unknowable, or what Bion designated O.

Eigen writes:

It is important to have filter systems for God—laws, angels, rituals, a messiah. Our mystical selves claim immediate contact with God. We have to live with our mystical selves a long time to get some sense of how to use that contact. What to do with mystical experience is a lifelong learning process. How can we use contact with God to enrich, not destroy? (p. 191)

Perhaps such questions are beyond being unanswerable; they may even be unbearable too. Yet there is a search for words. Listen to the poet Edmond Jabès (1987, p. 90), "I will tell you how being burrows various passages through the night of dreams towards the word."

It is impossible to separate the mystic Eigen from the pragmatic critical one or the expressive experimenting one. These passionate facets of the author's self coexist and strengthen each other. They contribute to a conviction that making a space for human suffering to emerge, respecting "naked psychic life ... for its own sake" (p. 137) allows the possibility of contacting the strength to truly *be*. When a space for suffering is opened, when one "comes through," first with disbelief, then again and again, then one can perhaps discover what the poet Allen Ginsburg sang: "The weight of the world / is love" (1959, p. 50).

Eigen (1993) has written:

> My underlying attitude was faith in the goodness of life, echoing God's appraisal of his work in *Bereishis* (*Genesis*). This is not an attitude that everyone shares, or that I always share with myself. Every moment is filled with myriad plus and minus aspects. In some instances, the plus seems faint indeed. (p. xx)

The larger questions of what we take to be true about human nature are rarely addressed. Yet doesn't it seem necessary to have a strong sense of the ultimate goodness of life in order to really risk going to those regions where the darkest aspects of the human mind may dwell, entrenched in hopelessness and despair? If such a sense of goodness and faith is the product of wishing, it will easily be blasted to bits by experience. Wishing is not enough. Eigen offers his readers a picture of the resilience of the person. Ultimately some sense of the goodness and creativity of psychic life potentially reveals itself if we can open to and bear the pain and terror of coming alive to psychic deadness. "Say what you will," writes the elder poet William Carlos Williams in introducing Allen Ginsburg's first book *Howl* (1959), "in spite of the most debasing experiences that life can offer a man, the spirit of love survives to ennoble our lives if we have the wit and the courage and the faith—and the art! to persist" (p. 8).

CHAPTER 3

The Obstructive Object

I N THIS ESSAY I EXPLORE THE CONCEPT OF AN INTERNAL object that perpetuates an atmosphere of intense mental pain, violence, and self-attack. Chronic self-attack, including attacks on linking, blocks the growth of a sense of personal agency that would ordinarily allow a person to receive help and to cooperate in her own analytic transformation. According to W. R. Bion, some patients give evidence of living with an internal object that is ego destructive and that operates as a *projective identification rejecting object.* Bion names this ego-destructive internal object an obstructive object.

In the following sections I will describe some implications of Bion's obstructive object idea. First I will explore the central theme of learning in Bion's psychology, giving special attention to the role of projective identification as a form of communication in earliest life. Next, I review Bion's ideas about the phenomenon of an obstructive object. I then offer a sketch of an *obstructive object scenario* as I am currently able to formulate it, offering a brief description from a case. Finally, I suggest that progress in working with the obstructive object scenario involves the analyst's capacity to become a *projective identification welcoming object* that the patient can use interpersonally and ultimately identify with.

The Scope of Bion's Work:
The Importance of Learning from Experience

Bion's writing can be profitably read as the evolution of twin psychologies: one about the conditions that sponsor learning and emotional development, and another about the myriad obstructive forces and conditions, both internal and environmental, that lead to psychological stalemate, breakdown, or malignant transformation. A tension between learning (in the widest sense the evolution of the mind) and obstruction to learning expands from Bion's early group work all the way through his final papers.

The roots of Bion's interest in learning are no doubt to be found in his own autobiography. Such a study is beyond the scope of this essay. However, even as a little boy Bion was a keen observer and a curious child. In his autobiography, *The Long Weekend* (1985), he gives us many moving vignettes about his curiosity, his sensitivity to his own emotional states as well as to those of others, his confusions over language, and his openness to impressions of all sorts.

Bion's war experience, which began when he was a teenager, provides a critical context for understanding the meaning that learning from experience came to have for him over the remainder of his deeply reflective life. He realized that groups (1961) can become anti-learning assemblages, and that failing to learn—indeed, failing to think—can be a matter of life and death. The anti-learning forces observable in groups can also be inferred in the individual personality. What I want to emphasize is that for Bion the theme of learning is not an academic one. Learning is about emotional experience. It can be detected in the movement from survival to creativity, from gathered information to personal realization, and from evacuative reaction to action mediated by reflective thought. Learning involves, in Bion's terms, the individual's relationship to the very fabric of life itself, attention (or its absence) to the emotional texture of truthful experience from which wisdom or folly may spring.

Bion explicitly distinguishes "learning from experience" from "learning about." For example, I may learn about psychoanalysis by reading books, seeing films, and listening to others who have been in analysis share their experiences. These experiences allow me to gather information and to form impressions about which I may have strong feelings. I may even come to believe I know a great deal about psychoanalysis. However, such learning can in no way substitute for the experience of actually participating in psychoanalysis. These two kinds of knowing give rise to a personal "language of achievement" in contradistinction

to the "language of substitution." The mind, according to Bion, only 乀⊃
grows when nourished by contact with truthfulness. The task of maturation is to grow a greater and deeper capacity to explore experience and
to become yet more truthful, to distinguish lies, and to make space to
recognize the thoughts that are seeking a thinker. Experience, especially
emotional experience, provides the building blocks of the mind.

How does this process of learning from experience take place?
Projective identification provides one model of what sponsors healthy
emotional development and learning from experience in earliest life.
Extending Klein's work, Bion (1962) introduces the idea of normal projective identification as a form of communication between a baby and
her mother (p. 37). The infant's facial expressions, vocalizations, crying,
and muscular gestures signal his distress. By distress I mean something
familiar: raw emotional experience at the level of sensation that obtrudes upon the infant's attention or awareness. This obtrusion may be
of such intensity that it saturates the infant's experience through states of
sensory-dominated arousal. Bion (1962) gives this familiar human experience a very abstract name. He calls such primitive sensory or emotional
distress beta elements (p. 6) According to Bion, beta elements are suit-
able only to be projected, or as he says, evacuated. This word—*evacuated*—speaks to the force and intensity of the process.

What is the fate of evacuated distress? Put more simply, what is the
fate of the infant's cry of pain? In order for distress to be transformed,
Bion suggests that it must find a home in the mind of another. Hopefully
a mind can be found to register the infant's pain. Still more importantly,
that mind should belong to an individual more emotionally mature—
someone with more experience of tolerating distress than the infant. If
this is so, then pain can be more than registered, it can be recognized,
reflected upon, and replied to creatively and compassionately.

Bion asks the question, What does this other mind do for the infant
in distress? Something helps the experience of raw emotional distress
become an opportunity to evolve in the direction of discovering meaning. Bion says this something that helps is called "alpha function." The
discovery of meaning depends upon the mother's ability to use her mind,
including her attention, intuition, and emotional experience (all factors
in her alpha function) to contain her infant's distress (the beta elements),

Beta → Alpha [handwritten]

and to transform that distress imaginatively.

In Bion's abstract formulation beta elements are transformed into alpha elements. Alpha elements are, according to Bion, the building blocks of memory, dreams, and reflective awareness. The capacity to learn from experience (Bion, 1962) depends upon a growing ability to transform beta elements into alpha elements. This transformation is sponsored as the infant internalizes and identifies with the mother as a containing object capable of alpha function.

According to Bion, an infant is dependent upon the actual separate mind of another in a particular way. The infant's needs for food, safety, proximity, and other forms of concrete care may be adequately provided for. Bion highlights another dimension of experience that he feels is an essential factor in the evolution of the infant's mind. An infant also depends upon the quality of mother's attention, and her capacity for reverie as a factor in alpha function. In short, the infant depends upon the unique qualities of the mother's own internal object world as expressed through the quality of her interactions with her baby. The quality of the mother's emotional presence helps her infant's mind to be born and to grow emotionally.

what about environment? [handwritten margin note]

A mother sponsors the essential experience of transformation from beta to alpha, from distress to comfort, repeatedly. She picks her baby up, rocks her, sings to her, and speaks aloud about what might be troubling her infant. She allows her infant to disengage when overstimulated and she reengages with her infant when her infant's gestures signal the desire to reconnect. The successful transformation of distress to comfort makes play and exploration possible. In essence, mother uses her own intuition, her unconscious memory of her own care as a child, and her emotional availability in the moment to investigate the experience of her infant and to reply to it.

According to Bion, the capacity to learn from experience is essentially characterized by an ability to tolerate and transform rather than to evade the inevitable turbulence and frustration of uncertain and painful situations. It also involves a faith that in states of distress—including even acute distress—one will not become totally trapped in an atmosphere of emotional catastrophe. Instead, this faith, based on the accumulated memories of the mother's repeated capacity to receive and transform distress into comfort, promotes a capacity for personal reverie, that is, a reverie for one's own experience as it arises and is lived through. This capacity for personal reverie can be pictured as the self's ability to turn toward and rely upon *internal projective identification welcoming objects* that can bear the turbulence of a new experience and can sponsor openness toward learning and exploration. The capacity for transformation from distress to comfort is the basis for motivated initiative. It requires continued rejuvenation, from both internal and external support, and must be widened, expanded, and continually consolidated as new experiences pressure the mind to grow.

The Obstructive Object and the Failure to Learn from Experience

By observing the phenomena of the obstructive object, a model can be developed for understanding why learning from experience seems nearly impossible for some people. Bion introduces the term "obstructive object" in his "schizophrenia" papers (1984), particularly in "On Arrogance" (1957) and "A Theory of Thinking" (1962). These papers, along with "Attacks on Linking" (1959), form the background for several passages from *Learning from Experience* that describe the consequences not only of a failure of maternal reverie and absent or inadequate alpha function, but also such important variables as an excess of envy as well as very low frustration tolerance in the infant. A constellation of factors of this kind can contribute to severe vulnerability in the mother–infant dyad. Such vulnerability may inhibit or obstruct the development of the container–contained relationship over time and make faith in the reliable transformation of distress to comfort impossible to realize.

The roots of the concept of the obstructive object are to be found in Klein's work on splitting and the paranoid-schizoid position. Klein focuses on the development of psychic reality through the mechanisms of introjection and projection. According to Linda Buckingham (2002), Klein theorized that

> Infants with an inherently low tolerance of frustration are likely to have phantasies of a bad, denying breast and will experience sadistic, attacking impulses towards it. This sets in train a negative

cycle: fears of retribution, introjection of a bad, damaged breast, feelings of persecution which are projected back into the breast, and so on. Early disjunction between mother and baby can set in even if the mother is doing her best to counteract the baby's anxiety. Another baby, with high tolerance of frustration, may thus fare better under worse external circumstances, although a baby whose mother is not in touch with her needs will suffer. (p. 207)

A close reading of Bion finds him extending Klein's work and carefully addressing the intersection of interpersonal and intrapsychic variables that may give rise to situations that he names "infantile catastrophe" and "nameless dread." Bion suggests that for some patients distress is never reliably transformed and that dire consequences follow.

In "Attacks on Linking," Bion (1959) writes:

Projective identification makes it possible for him to investigate his own feelings in a personality powerful enough to contain them. Denial of the use of this mechanism, either by the refusal of the mother to serve as a repository for the infant's feelings, or by the hatred and envy of the patient who cannot allow the mother to exercise this function, leads to a destruction of the link between infant and breast and consequently to a severe disorder of the impulse to be curious *on which all learning depends.* The way is therefore prepared for a severe arrest of development. Furthermore, thanks to a denial of the main method open to the infant for dealing with his too powerful emotions, the conduct of emotional life, in any case a severe problem, becomes intolerable. Feelings of hatred are thereupon directed against all emotions including hate itself, and against external reality which stimulates them. It is a short step from hatred of the emotions to hatred of life itself. (pp. 107–08, emphasis added)

Here Bion is going a step beyond both Freud and Klein. Instead of positioning the individual's main conflict as arising between reality and fantasy or between love and hate or between the life instincts and the death instinct, Bion describes how some patients are faced with a choice between emotion and anti-emotion. In the absence of maternal reverie or in the presence of excessive envy or frustration, hatred is directed toward emotional experience itself.

A critical feature of the obstructive object relationship is that the person feels overwhelmed by emotional experience. According to the *American Heritage Dictionary* (1981), one meaning of distress is "the condition of being in need of immediate assistance." This definition seems to capture the experience of the infant who feels a desperate urgency for relief when raw emotional experience (beta elements) obtrudes upon awareness. Bion (1977) writes:

> If there are only beta-elements, which cannot be made unconscious, there can be no repression, suppression, or learning. This creates the impression that the patient is incapable of discrimination. He cannot be unaware of any single sensory stimulus: yet such hypersensitivity is not contact with reality. (p. 8)

It is at this very moment of distress and vulnerability that a containing object is so desperately needed. What kind of object will be there to greet the infant's distress? The obstructive object, as defined by Bion, is overwhelming in a quite particular way. An obstructive object is a projective identification rejecting object that has been internalized. Bion (1959) writes:

> The [infant's] rudimentary consciousness cannot carry the burden placed upon it (by the experience of uncontained distress). The establishment of a projective-identification-rejecting-object means that instead of an understanding object the infant has a wilfully misunderstanding object—with which it is identified. (p. 117)

I want to unpack Bion's condensed language and try to bring closer to home what I think he intends to describe. What does a projective identification rejecting object look like and feel like? In infant observation or in clinical work with mothers and infants one can sometimes painfully observe the interpersonal origins of the obstructive object. Imagine, for example, an infant crying in his crib. Mother for some reason cannot bear her baby's crying. She does not pick her baby up and try to sooth him. Instead, she leaves the room, perhaps shutting the door to muffle her baby's cries. This is a literal description of a scenario in which the baby's distress is rejected. Bion suggests that this sort of scenario leaves the baby in a state of potentially unmodified distress. Drawing on the experience of infant observation, I can speculate about the sorts of experiences that a baby might have after its projective identification of distress has been rejected. Suppose that one could observe this baby now left alone in its crib. Perhaps the infant will cry until exhausted and then withdraw into sleep. Perhaps he will adhesively identify with a pattern on the curtain or a shadow on the wall as a way of fixing his attention and subjectively pulling himself together. Perhaps we can imagine him finding his thumb, putting it into his mouth, sucking, and in this way gradually calming. Perhaps he will become muscularly tense and rigid, curling his toes, making his fingers into fists, stiffening his neck and arching his back and finally settling into a different state. Now imagine that this scenario is repeated many times over several weeks or months without variation. A great deal depends, of course, on the complexity of the patterns of communication and rejection that are unfolding, evolving, or reifying between mother and baby over time. Somehow these patterns become unconsciously represented by both partners in terms of unconscious relational expectations (Beebe and Lachmann, 2002).

It is from patterns of this kind that one can begin to appreciate what an obstructive object creating scenario looks like and feels like. My contention is that an obstructive object scenario is a more extreme and chronic outcome of the repeated experience of meeting the other as a projective identification rejecting object. I want to be clear that I think the creation of the obstructive object scenario involves vulnerability at both the intrapsychic and the interpersonal levels of experience. This scenario takes different forms with varying intensities for different patients. For the sake of brevity, I want to simplify the situation to its essentials. The obstructive object relationship, according to Bion, is "wilfully misunderstanding." I am interested in conveying the feel of this kind of link.

Imagine, now, a mother who cannot stand her infant's crying. She feels, for her own unconscious reasons, that her infant is *doing something to her* by crying out in distress. This mother cannot bear what feels too overwhelming. She screams at her infant to shut up. Maybe she shakes her infant to silence him. In the worst of all scenarios, she suffocates her infant with a pillow to silence him. An obstructive object is experienced as someone or something actively hostile toward emotional experience creating an atmosphere of escalating pressure and violence. Although it is beyond the scope of this paper to describe, it is my experience that the obstructive object scenario is created anew again and again over generations.   *Transgenerational abuse...*

Another way to picture the obstructive object is by turning to myth. For example, following Bion, the figure of the Sphinx is emblematic of an obstructive object. When we remember the Sphinx, we remember a monster. She is part woman, part lion, and part bird. We also remember her riddle. What is much more important than the content of her riddle, however, is the emotionally violent atmosphere evoked when the Sphinx stops Oedipus from continuing on his journey. There is an atmosphere of intense threat, confusion, and hatred. The Sphinx is not felt to be asking riddles playfully, or in the service of learning, but in a bizarre and violent manner, as weapons to attack links and thinking.

Recall the images from the Oedipus myth. The Sphinx blocks the road to Thebes, stopping everyone who wishes to enter. She demands that they answer a riddle in order to pass. She threatens people by saying that if they answer her wrongly they will die. The obstructive object sponsors an atmosphere of confusion and terror. The subject is faced with an unconscious choice between omnipotence or helpless collapse.   *Protest or despair*   This dire choice is symbolized by the Sphinx's own suicide when Oedipus guesses a plausible answer to the riddle. One is left in an atmosphere of horror.

With these images in mind, one can begin to observe a certain category of phenomena in the consulting room that superficially appear to be motivated by destructive impulses. It is very important to differentiate the consequences of violent projections, which are, indeed, often   *yes*   destructive, from their motivation, which may be very different. The intensity and pervasiveness of some forms of violent projection may be part of an unconsciously frantic search for a helping object that can transform

[handwritten: & relief = violent projectic]

pain and distress into comfort. If relief is not adequately found, the violence of the projection intensifies. Such constant and intense projections may then serve multiple simultaneous functions. The projection may serve to get rid of pain through evacuation; it may serve to communicate distress still more emphatically; or it may serve to try to control an object through an invasive fantasy, what Klein originally called excessive projective identification. Or it may serve to destroy the mental apparatus through a process described by Bion as "attacks on links." Since none of these functions can lead to an adequate transformation of distress into comfort, the self is faced with overwhelming emotional experiences that over time produce an atmosphere of intense ego-destructive dread.

Bion (1959) gives this description from his own clinical work in his essay, "Attacks on Linking":

> Associations from a period in the analysis...showed an increasing intensity of emotions in the patient. This originated in what he felt was my refusal to accept parts of his personality. Consequently he strove to force them into me with increased desperation and violence. His behaviour, isolated from the context of the analysis, might have appeared to be an expression of primary aggression. The more violent his phantasies of projective identification, the more frightened he became of me. There were sessions in which such behaviour expressed unprovoked aggression, but I quote this...because it shows the patient in a different light, his violence a reaction to what he felt was my hostile defensiveness. (p. 104)

The Obstructive Object in the Clinical Encounter

Over the past several years, I have tried to observe what might be called an obstructive object scenario in my clinical work with children and adults. One feature I have noticed is the phenomenon of constant and intense projection as serving a crucial function in perpetuating the overwhelming aspect of the obstructive object. Often we think of projective identification arising as a discrete response to an overwhelmingly intense experience. However, in my experience, some patients rely upon a kind of pervasive projective identification. Because distress cannot be transformed into comfort, some people act as if their minds have become machines for evacuation. Constant and intense projections blur the already tenuous boundary between self and other. This pervasive projection creates an atmosphere of confusion, hostility, and agitated frustration because intense distress is felt to be always already present everywhere.

I have learned much about the obstructive object scenario by working with a patient I'll call Paula. Paula is a middle-aged woman who feels unable to sustain a loving sexual relationship with a man over time, or to complete her professional and educational ambitions, and unable to earn a satisfactory income. She is highly intelligent but blocked in her capacity to learn from experience. She says she has no confidence in herself. Until recently she had given little thought to her future.

Upon entering analysis, Paula characterized her daily experience as "scattered," "foggy," and "dreamlike." After several years of our working together, Paula is able to observe how she "constantly distracts herself from the moment." She now reports finding some sense of being able to "be clear" and "to think straight." Paula still seems to oscillate between states of hyperarousal (sometimes reaching a level of panic) and hypoarousal (feeling exhausted, depressed, and sometimes overwhelmed with despair). She is still often exhausted by what feels to her like an unrelenting assaulting present from which she cannot escape.

Paula's early sessions were filled with fragmented descriptions of her feelings of deep rage and disturbance about the many atrocities occurring throughout the world. Paula seemed to repeat the same fragmented stories, often in detail, as if she had never seen me before or as if she could not believe I was listening to her or remembering our meetings.

Very quickly I began to wonder if Paula could listen to me. Things I said seemed to be willfully ignored. Paula felt intensely disturbed by what she said was evidence of the corruption of the Bush administration. She also felt persecuted by the men in charge at her workplace. I understood these complaints at one level as a gathering of the transference, but Paula rejected transference interpretations as formulaic and "psychoanalytic bullshit." Paula insisted on the merit of her concrete concerns, especially of the shared social situation we were both living through.

I often felt intimidated, rejected, angry, and exhausted in the face of Paula's tirades. Her seeming unwillingness to accept my sincere attempts at understanding began to wear me down day after day. Over time she became worried that I could not see or acknowledge her worries about "the real world." She implied that I was the one who needed analysis and that I was ill because I could not acknowledge reality.

Eventually I began to recognize that Paula might unconsciously experience every emotional relationship as an obstructive object scenario. I began to discern that I might be enacting a role that seemed to feel to Paula like a projective identification rejecting object. Through self-analysis and supervision I tried to open up my way of thinking about being with Paula in order to be more at-one with her picture of the world. I realized that Paula seemed to believe that I was a willfully misunderstanding object trying to force my illness into her.

With many patients, I often experience a greater or lesser degree of what I regard as reverie. By reverie I mean an openness and freedom to listen to myself listening to the patient (Grotstein, personal communication, 2003). In any given session the emotional experience of being with a patient may evoke sensations, images, memories, reflections, or sudden intuitive hunches that can become part of the material that eventually forms an interpretation. The capacity to be in reverie sponsors a kind of inquiry into and spontaneous description of the emotional field arising between patient and analyst in the moment. With Paula I felt little freedom to speak much less to dream the session, nor to let my mind relax, wander, or play. Instead, I often felt "on the edge of my seat" (sometimes literally) because of the tension in the room. I expected Paula to explode and sometimes she did.

The question, I think, that faced me in working with Paula was how to be in two places simultaneously. Paula seemed to regard me as the embodiment of a willfully misunderstanding object, amplifying her distress with my apparently cruel and stupid interpretations. I had to find some way to accept this reality in the transference. At the same time, I began to ask myself how I could become the opposite of an obstructive object, a projective identification welcoming object. How could I do this in a way that would feel real to Paula? How could I find a place in myself where I could tolerate the distress aroused in me by being with her? I had to try to find my way toward my own projective identification welcoming objects in order to tolerate, contain, and transform my own significant distress so that a space of reverie could become tenuously possible. I think the key point here is the idea that working through in the countertransference involves repeatedly reestablishing and contacting the vitality of one's own projective identification welcoming objects rather than giving in to the temptation to slam the door on the potential of living through and transforming both the analyst's and the patient's distress. Each of us has to find our own ways, through experience, to make this kind of opening up to pain possible. The personal obstacles to allowing this kind of development can be significant indeed.

The Welcoming Object and the Transformation of Pain

How does an infant realize a mother's reverie? I suggest that the mother in reverie helps to facilitate a transformation that in its most primitive form is subjectively registered by the infant as moving from bodily distress to bodily comfort. In the actual beginning of the infant's life, the transformation from beta elements to alpha elements involves a feeling of somatic relief. Before the infant has the capacity to represent this transformation in organized images, I suggest that the infant experiences the shape of this transformation in bodily experiences of calming and relaxation. The capacity of the infant to become calm after a state of anxious arousal is, I suggest, one of the earliest and most important transformations repeatedly facilitated by a mother in reverie. It may be that this first transformation is already developing in fetal life. Whenever it occurs, I name this transformation, descriptively, a transformation from distress to comfort.

An infant able to receive and use a mother's reverie is gradually able to experience psychical qualities, whereas an infant for some reason deprived of the benefit of reverie may remain trapped within the intensity and concreteness of distress. A projective identification welcoming object promotes the recognition of psychical experience and the presence of a space for thinking, while a projective identification rejecting object leads to a denial or even hatred of psychic reality. A projective identification welcoming object is the basis for the establishment of the evolving relationship between container and contained that promotes the transformation of distress to comfort.

The mother's capacity for reverie and her ability to lend her alpha function to her infant's state of distress is a comfort that strengthens her infant's developing mind through the creation of alpha elements that eventually make the comprehension of meaningful emotional experience possible. The provision of alpha function not only brings relief, but also the possibility of a new experience, a novel and evolving relationship to distress that over the process of maturation becomes represented in increasingly sophisticated ways. Also at stake is the fate of attention. The infant trapped in distress dissociates its attention from more and more experience, while an infant capable of the transformation from distress to comfort establishes a curious link to other objects and is free to explore experience.

My challenge was to find a way to make real for Paula the experience of this earliest transformation from distress to comfort in order to help her mind to grow freer to learn from emotional experience. Somehow, as I have said, I had to free my own mind to allow more room for observation, reverie, play, and exploration. So, what did I do? First, I began to slow down, to say less, and to try to be at-one with Paula's experience rather than trying to describe something about the transference between us. This seemed to help. Gradually the atmosphere of the sessions began to change. Paula's complaints came nearer to home, and focused upon her parents and siblings. Why should this be so? It seems to me that I was literally making space for Paula's distress to exist, in her, within me, and between us. Before it could be transformed, spaces had to be discovered where her distress could be tolerated. During this time Paula began to describe the way she could feel that her distress was really registered by me and that this felt like a disorientingly new experience.

Over time, Paula began to bring more dreams. Some of her dreams were horrific. Her dreams began to picture intensely shaming objects, both male and female. These objects were not only willfully misunderstanding, but cruel and annihilating. My sense is that our work allowed the obstructive object to begin to take shape in her dream life so that we could begin to face it together. For reasons of confidentiality, I am not reporting Paula's dreams. However, I will share the dream of another

patient because it so beautifully pictures the movement from the domi-
nation of the obstructive object to the tentative discovery of a projective
identification welcoming object:

> A small figure approaches a larger figure. The small figure carries
> in her arms a large red-hot burning coal. The coal has burned
> away the hands and arms of the small figure up to the elbows.
> The small figure desperately wants to pass the coal to the larger
> figure but is afraid of injuring the larger figure and of how the
> larger figure will react.

This dream poignantly illustrates the awakening of a search for a projective identification welcoming object, and beautifully portrays the experience of raw emotional distress. The red-hot coal represents emotional
intensity that is too searing to bear. A passage from John Lampen (1987),
a Quaker essayist, gives imaginative voice to the small figure of this
dream. This is the sort of thing I think a patient can begin to put into
words when they feel in touch with a projective identification welcoming
object:

> I need you to take this great lump of pain which I feel.... I want
> you to look at it, and feel it, and think about it. Perhaps you can
> blunt some of its edges, soften it a little with your tears, or throw
> it up in the air and catch it to show me it is not so heavy as I
> thought. Perhaps you can take a measure and show me its proper
> size. Perhaps you could just hold it a little, while I get back on my
> feet again. But then you should give it back to me, because it is
> my load and my task. You may carry away a little of the poison,
> but the real task of making it safe can only be done by me. (p. 29)

The discovery of a projective identification welcoming object sponsors
the yearning to live and experience and to learn despite intense suffering. Paula has begun to express a tentative but powerful sense of being
in love with love. This love is so fragile and so painful that it hurts to
acknowledge it. She describes not only being terrified of an objectively
dangerous and brutal world outside, but also, and even more intensely,

of a loss of her sense of the emerging preciousness of experience when the old persecutory relationship within herself reappears. All of Paula's critiques of "the real world" apparently served as screens to deflect our attention from her terrible anxiety of being someone who hates and fears her own emotional experience while at the same time desperately yearning to be more open to experience.

Paula's sense of humor has been of immense help to us both. She has a kind of gallows humor that makes space to face the immense pain of her life. She has begun to be interested in spiritual questions and has even started to wonder about the meaning of her life in ways that she had never engaged before. Analysis seems to be helping Paula to begin to symbolize her experience, particularly the presence of the cruel obstructive object. Recognizing and facing this cruel obstructive object seems sometimes unbearably intimidating. What has been especially important to us both has been the growing capacity for compassion that seems to arise as space is made to observe and describe the ways that her psychic reality is structured around approaching and withdrawing from the violent internal projective identification rejecting object. The more I can clearly and emotionally describe this situation, the more I gradually earn Paula's tentative trust. We have both begun to experience a kind of *living through hell* together. It seems that I *must* experience the feelings of rage, frustration, hopelessness, and helplessness that emerge while trying to think and experience in the presence of an obstructive object. Being more at-one with Paula's experience is necessary in order to really begin to find words that feel truthful to her and that can hold her attention and reorient her to a new kind of relationship.

Concluding Thoughts

This paper has suggested that one of the most painful situations in analytic work involves the obstructive object relationship first described by Bion. The practical task of psychoanalysis is to identify, describe, and over time to transform the unconscious modes of coping with pain that were learned very early in life and that can be observed in transferences into the present. Our task is to learn to describe—and in doing so, contain and bring awareness to—the shifting levels of pain and anxiety that the patient experiences, moment to moment and session to session. Over time, the mindfulness and reverie that we demonstrate for our patient are internalized and become part of the patient's own projective identification welcoming object world. These more creative internal object relationships can be increasingly relied upon to sponsor learning from experience over the course of a lifetime.

There are particular challenges in working with obstructive object scenarios. Patients block introjection of the therapist's alpha function because of their own pervasive projective identification. They anticipate rejection and attack because they are identified with an ego-destructive internal object. The analyst has the large challenge of bearing the strain of the Sphinx-like encounter with terror and dread that the patient experiences upon emerging into an obstructive object transference that often has been deeply split off and denied. By avoiding the trap of concretely enacting a projective identification rejecting object, the analyst, through his actual reverie and presence with the patient, gives the patient an experience that stimulates her own alpha function and in the best situations allows mourning and the working through of depressive anxieties to take place. This in turn sponsors the reclamation of attention and thwarted life instincts, which may now revive and expand by relying upon the new experience of a projective identification welcoming object and a sense of relationship to one's own internal world. Through successful analytic work, one can observe how the patient withdraws her projections from external objects back into herself and her internal objects. This process happens as she begins to discover the analyst as a containing object, one who welcomes projective identifications rather than rejecting them as anticipated.

The Permanent Earthquake:
Notes on the Treatment of a Young Boy

For what am "I" but a colony of souls, of whom now one and now another gets hold of the communal consciousness? And what I call "myself" is the net product of the activity of many selves, the harmony, or discord (whichever the case may be) of a number of contrapuntal personalities.

— Aldous Huxley "The Critic in the Crib"

O VER THE PAST SEVERAL YEARS IN THE UNITED States, there has been a dramatic increase of interest in the diagnosis, treatment, and understanding of autism, Asperger's syndrome, and autistic spectrum disorders. A variety of treatments are now advocated but a psychodynamic approach is rarely considered a preferred intervention by most providers. By contrast, in England and other places, interest in the psychodynamic treatment of children with autism and Asperger's syndrome has begun to flourish during the same period (see, for instance, Acquarone and Raphael-Leff, 2007; Alvarez, 1992; Alvarez and Reid, 1999; Edwards, 2001; Rhode and Klauber, 2004). Frances Tustin has provided inspiration and furthered the work of many psychotherapists working psychodynamically with autistic spectrum disorders. Recent collections (Houzel and Rhode, 2005; J. Mitrani and T. Mitrani, 1997; Tremelloni, 2005) pay homage to Tustin's seminal influence both directly and indirectly. Her pioneering work highlights the central importance of finding ways of making emotional contact with difficult-to-reach children in order to foster an opportunity for growth and development to gradually become possible. Tustin's (1992) compassion and creativity are evident when she writes:

As therapists, we have to establish ourselves as alive human beings who, by establishing co-operative enterprises with the psychotic child, can help him to regulate and pattern such feelings
because we are in touch with these elemental depths both in ourselves and in him. As he feels taken care of by people who can
withstand his domineering, monopolizing attacks, he will feel
potential rivals are similarly kept in order. As he begins to feel
less open to attack, the use of autistic objects will diminish. His
openings will become places where fulfilling connections can be
made instead of being places which need to be blocked against
the entry of inimical substances. He will begin to realize that
they are places where healing influences can come in. (p. 148)

Tustin has given us a window into the complex psychic reality that can
emerge in some children when conditions have been established for
communication. Her work makes it possible to glimpse the complexity
of mental experience sometimes going on behind autistic barriers.

My intention here is to share my experience as a psychotherapist
working psychodynamically with autistic states of mind. Inspired by
Tustin's example, I describe my work with a boy I shall call Eric. I explore, through clinical material, this eight-year-old boy's movement from
the agony of consciousness to the expanding awareness of consciousness.
Through several vignettes I will attempt to portray the arc of a treatment, showing some of the openings in Eric's experience that allowed
for "fulfilling connections" to evolve. I hope to show how the impact
of discovering the externality of another human being, developing the
capacity for sharing attention, and learning how to play all gradually become sources of the healing influence that allowed Eric to move from a
very narrow and constricted experience to a much wider awareness, even
to coming into contact with a colony of souls within.

History

Eric is the firstborn child of Carol and Martin. He has one sister four
years younger. In my initial meetings with Eric's parents, Carol described her pregnancy as uncomplicated, but said that at birth she nearly

pre-natal
experience horror!
3 x loss
4 "death" in life...
literal

bled to death after Eric was delivered. It seems that Eric had a twin who died sometime during the pregnancy and this fact complicated the delivery of the placenta. As a result of this traumatic situation Carol was exhausted, and her medical recovery took several days.

Carol described Eric as an extraordinarily beautiful baby even though she said that "he never made eye contact with anyone but me." She said that he was hypersensitive and averse to sounds and touch from the very beginning. Eric was breast fed and weaning was not accomplished until the age of three. As Eric began to crawl and walk, he was often very clumsy and banged into things. Eric began talking early. Carol said that he loved words and that he talked constantly to the point of irritating others. Carol reported that she had Eric evaluated by a local program; ultimately he began sensory integration treatment involving physical therapy and some speech and language therapy at around the age of five. She believed these treatments helped with Eric's coordination and with his sense of confidence. She also credited modifications in his diet, like eliminating wheat, corn, and dairy products, as having a favorable impact on his mood. Eric had also taken various levels of Paxil during the time I met with him.

When four months old, Eric developed a high fever and was hospitalized for several days. He was diagnosed with a bladder infection. Carol said that she stayed with him at the hospital and he would calm only if she held him. She believed that Eric might have died from his infection and wonders if this might have permanently impacted his personality. She recalled the episode as "torturous" and said that Eric had never been the same after this experience.

Early in my work with Eric, Carol provided a report from a neuropsychological exam. The report stated:

> Eric is…a boy with a long history of developmental and motor delays and significant behavior difficulties. Behavior concerns include poor impulse control, irritability, aggression, explosive anger outbursts, obsessive qualities and impaired social skills. School adjustment problems appeared as early as Kindergarten. Eric is currently home schooled. Diagnostic considerations include sensory integration disorder, ADHD, depression, affective

and disruptive problems, Asperger's Syndrome, and Pervasive Developmental Disorder.

The report's summary concluded:

> Comprehensive neuropsychological examination describes a child whose test taking behavior suggested significant ADHD features (i.e., impulsivity, short attention span, distractibility, restlessness, impatience, hyperactivity, low frustration tolerance). Most striking, however, were his very high levels of intensity and over-focus.

I recommended that Eric be seen four times per week. This recommendation seemed unrealistic to both parents for financial, practical, and emotional reasons. A schedule of twice-weekly sessions was agreed upon and this schedule was maintained with additional sessions occasionally added until the end of treatment (over almost five years).

Early Sessions

The toys to be chosen from in my playroom include wooden blocks, Legos, a dollhouse and several family figures, a small sand tray with a large number of animals, soldiers, dinosaurs, trees, cars, and various other objects. I also offer puppets, soft balls, and art supplies, including colored pencils, crayons, pens, string, scissors, tape, and glue. While most of the toys are shared, each child receives his or her own box of personal art supplies. This represents a modification of the classic Kleinian play situation.

My approach to patients, including children, begins as an observational one. My priority is to try to follow the child's behavior; to understand his motivations, anxieties, and emotions; and to establish a situation where deepening communication is possible. Because communication is so often obstructed in the beginning of treatment with children like Eric, I focus my attention on listening to myself listening to the child, experiencing myself experiencing the child, and I try to use the impact of the unfolding link between us (or the lack of a link) to help me guess what might be developing in the child's experience and, eventually, in the experience shared between us. I'm particularly interested in how the child reacts to my presence. Finding words to describe the moment-to-moment unfolding of the experience of the presence of another human mind may woo the child's attention away from his own isolating activities toward becoming interested in shared experience.

In our first meeting Eric came into the consulting room, walked to the window, and without looking at me gazed outside for awhile. He kept his back to me. I don't remember what I said but in any case he didn't respond. I noticed that he twisted his fingers rapidly. He occasionally jerked a little bit as if he had experienced a jolt of electricity. After a few minutes he went and crouched between the end of my couch and the wall. I had the intuition not to try to speak to him, so I sat down on the floor across the room from him where he could keep an eye on me. Mostly he didn't look at me.

Eventually Eric decided to move out into the middle of the room. I simply described to him that his curiosity must now be stronger than the feeling that he didn't really know who I was or what I was going to do. He seemed to tolerate this description. I then said something else about what he might be feeling. He briefly looked at me, laughed in an odd explosive ha!, and then rolled on his back, pulling his legs over his head. Then he picked his nose and ate the contents as he rocked back and forth.

I sensed that there was a provocative element in Eric's behavior. There seemed to be an enormous complexity in him that nonetheless was hard to observe and gain access to. Tustin's differentiation of the entangled confusional child from the encapsulated child (Tustin, 1986) has helped me to think about this complexity. She writes:

> Schizophrenic-type children (or confusional entangled children, as I call them) are very open and tell us about their strange misconceptions quite clearly. The encapsulated autistic children are very different in that they are closed up and secretive. It is difficult to feel sure about what one has inferred... (p. 40)

Tustin also points out that while confusional entangled children know some degree of bodily separateness and seek objects, encapsulated children seek sensations through the creation of autistic shapes and autistic hard objects. She also notes that projective identification operates in the confusional entangled child while it is felt not to operate in the encapsulated child. I felt that Eric might have elements of both encapsulating and entangling processes operating simultaneously. There were times when I felt contact with Eric might be more possible, while at other times he felt more shut off to me and I felt more shut out.

One day Eric came into the session and roamed aimlessly around the room. He stopped at the bookcase and ran his fingers up and down the spines of the books on the shelf. I imagined that this was not a purely sensory-dominated activity, and that Eric might be thinking something as he touched the books even though he seemed very far away. After awhile I said "It seems you have a worried look on your face." Without looking at me, he shrugged. I said "Maybe it's hard to find words to describe a worried feeling." He shrugged again. After awhile I said, "Maybe you prefer not to try to speak for some reason." Eric was quiet but then suddenly said "I'm always worried about something at the back of my mind."

The way Eric said the phrase "at the back of my mind" stimulated a strong reaction in me. In my reverie, the back of Eric's mind looked like an actual place where things were continuously happening. I wondered out loud if he could tell me more about what was going on in the back of his mind. He said, "Did you know that when I walk down the street I always look seven paces ahead in every direction?" This communication sounded odd to me. I thought it was not really addressed to me, but more to the world at large. He demonstrated, turning his head a little bit with each step, as if his head were a camera mounted on a moving robot body. I was surprised by this vivid performance. It did not, however, feel like play. Eric seemed to be showing (me) something he was very serious about. I wondered why he felt he must be so "vigilant." Eric said he liked the sound of the word "vigilant." I realized he probably didn't know what this word meant. I encouraged him to tell me more about what it is that he is looking for when he looks seven paces ahead. He said simply "I don't know."

Upon reflection I see a pattern in these early sessions. There were moments of moving toward and moments of turning away. There was an oscillation between seeking contact and caution, between risking communication and escaping back into isolation. I felt strongly that Eric wanted to communicate while at the same time feeling deeply ambivalent about how to do so. I felt intuitively that I might unintentionally be blocking Eric's desire to be in contact with me somehow. I made it a point to wonder to myself about my own role in obstructing Eric's attempts at knowing me and being known.

Eric and I experienced occasional "moments of meeting," one of the terms introduced by Daniel Stern and his colleagues (Stern et al., 1998). Using Stern's language, this session with Eric shows a series of "present moments," centering first on Eric's experience of "worry," then on the impact of his phrase "at the back of my mind," then the demonstration of his "looking seven paces ahead," and finally his experience of the word "vigilant." Each of these moments of contact moves our process along toward future, richer "now moments" (Stern) of emotional discovery and recognition.

During these early months, I explored a strategy of trying to catch the moments when Eric would come out and express himself. My noticing his fleeting signals of curiosity, emotion, and initiative was key, I think, in helping Eric make contact and tolerate the emergence of shared emotional experience. I wanted to try to help him tolerate and extend the experience of sharing contact with me. This took a lot of patience, guesswork, and attention. I felt I could neither intrude upon him nor leave him completely alone in his own world. I found an image from a supervisor helpful. I began to think of my attention as if it were a large fishing net cast into the sea of the session. My task, as I understood it, was to patiently troll for moments of potential emotional contact. I worked hard on slowing down, following Eric's lead when I could detect it, and deepening my capacity to observe what was gradually gathered in the net of awareness.

These were the first steps toward what Tustin has called "becoming rooted." As Tustin (1992) puts it:

> Clinical work which is informed by the infantile transference indicates that the constellation of nipple and tongue working

rhythmically together with mouth and breast sets the feeling of rootedness in train. As well as demonstrating the situation to us, the infantile transference enables the 'unrooted' (or 'uprooted') patient to become rooted. This basic sense of being rooted [in re-↘ lationship] sets the scene for the development of a sense of identity, security, and self confidence. (p. 32)

Becoming rooted, in Tustin's sense, involves the capacity for sharing experience, and for making contact through interaction with the mind of another. Through this contact one begins to sense the possibilities opened by such shared experience with a live-minded subject. Stern, in a very different conceptual scheme, has described the sequence of "moving along," "now moments," and "moments of meeting." Both Stern and Tustin are, in their own ways, seeking language to describe a "floor for experience" that can become, as Tustin describes it, "a rhythm of safety" and in Stern's language a new form of "implicit relational knowing."

Becoming Rooted

For the first several months of treatment Eric used verbal language sparingly. He was clearly capable of speaking, yet for some reason he often did not. He often communicated through action and the use of his body. He would come into the consulting room, flop on the couch, and begin rocking back and forth. Sometimes he banged his head on the back of the couch and laughed in an eerie way. I never felt that he was only trying to shut me out by doing this. I felt he was trying to evoke something in me, though I felt quite confused about what kind of message he might be trying to send. It was interesting to learn from his parents that he rarely behaved in this way at home.

Sometimes he would crawl between the couch and the wall, or into the middle of the room onto the small carpet there. He would become lost in the carpet's design, curl into a fetal position, and trace the patterns with his finger. I hypothesized to myself that, although sensation dominated, these actions were object related. In other words, I felt Eric had an intention to communicate something behind his action, and that he was seeking an audience, so to speak. I felt, in fact, that Eric was trying to "make a scene." Noticing this scene-making activity seemed important if I was to help Eric learn to share his experience. I reasoned that as important as the content of the scene might become, the first step was to notice the elements of a scene trying to be made, and that he was using his body as a vehicle of communication. I felt Eric wanted someone to witness the scene he was making, and perhaps to describe it, though not necessarily to become a part of it.

I saw my activity of trying to notice Eric's intentions in "making a scene" as another element of facilitating the process of making contact, albeit in a subtly complex way. As a step toward sharing experience, I needed to witness Eric's potential expressiveness without assuming any desire on his part for me to actively participate in his elaboration of a scene. What was shared, then, was not the scene-making activity itself, but rather his awareness of my attention to his activity. I was, as it were, an audience that he knew existed but that he did not have to attend to immediately and from moment to moment.

One day, while lying on the carpet like a little baby, Eric said that he was beginning to see pictures in the carpet. I asked him what kind of pictures he was seeing. He replied, in an agitated way, "I don't want to have to jump into the fire to burn up my feelings." I waited but he didn't say more. I said that I thought I understood what a dilemma it was to feel one's feelings are so intense that they will burn you up, or that you have to burn them away as the only way to deal with them. He became calm and relaxed for a period. Then he suddenly closed his eyes, grimaced, stuck out his tongue, and made claws with his hands and shrieked. Since I had no idea what this meant I said to him, "I wonder what that was?" He said, "A surprise!" I said "I wonder if those feelings came from somewhere in you and surprised you. Or maybe you were trying to surprise me?" He said quickly, "Both!" I regard these kinds of shared experiences as building up "a rhythm of safety" and a "container–contained" relationship through here-and-now experience and interaction. While I did not understand the content of Eric's unconscious phantasy, at another level its potential for meaning seemed to originate in his increasing ability to express and externalize a spontaneous emotional experience in my presence and even to address me directly.

Now Moments

Stern and his colleagues (1998) have introduced the term "now moments" to indicate "a special kind of 'present moment' that gets lit up subjectively and affectively, pulling one more fully into the present" (p. 911). Stern says of the now moment that it is "pregnant with an unknown future that can feel like an impasse or an opportunity" (p. 911). As he describes it,

> The present becomes very dense subjectively as in a "moment of truth." …The analyst intuitively recognizes that a window of opportunity for some kind of therapeutic reorganization or derailment is present, and the patient may recognize that he has arrived at a watershed in the therapeutic relationship. (p. 912)

Stern's notion of a now moment has a powerful descriptive appeal. In work with autistic children I have become particularly interested in the forms of proto-attention that may eventually lead to now moments. I think the movement toward being "now-here" versus "nowhere" is very important; its emergence seems to indicate a rudimentary first step toward the eventual recognition of the kind of now moment Stern has described. In this connection, I now want to describe a series of moments with Eric that seem to me to have moved our work forward over time. For me, they all indicate the movement from nowhere to now-here, and they are on the way toward now moments in which Eric can more fully recognize himself and my separate presence as well as the experience of sharing experience together.

In one session Eric was lying on the floor and began to move his arm and hand in a smooth, wavelike motion. I asked Eric if he had any thoughts while he was moving his hand and arm or if he just liked the feeling of the motion. He said that he had thoughts but that he didn't want to tell them now. I said that that was okay with me. Later I told him I had a feeling he was interested in the smoothness of the motion and talking about it probably felt like getting in the way of feeling the smoothness. Eric sat up and was quiet for a long time. He seemed to be "elsewhere." Then he said "May I ask you a question?" I said "Yes." He said, "Why is this room so beautiful? I have never been in such a beautiful place as here." I was stunned by this. I asked him what in particular gave him the sense of something being beautiful. Eric replied "Everything." I observed that the beauty seemed connected to feeling free now from too many worries. I said that maybe being together made him feel open to something new that might feel beautiful. Looking back I think Eric was experiencing the dawning of awareness of being in a now-here moment of relationship that felt mysterious and awesome. This certainly was how it felt to me, noticing his impact on my own emotional state.

Some months further into our work Eric came to a session in a state of acute distress. He exploded through the doorway screaming and charging at me. He smashed into me and began hitting and kicking me. I had no idea why. All I could do initially was to literally push him away, but he charged at me again and again. I simply repeated over and over to him, "I'm not going to hurt you and I'm not going to let you hurt me." Eric was screaming "I'm going to kill you. Let me out of here. You're going to die if you don't let me go home now!" He lived out this ferocious tantrum through much of the session. His physical intensity had a powerful effect on me. I found it hard to think. I felt disoriented, a little bit frightened, and increasingly angry. I thought about actually needing to protect myself and Eric. I remembered the way, early in my training while working with psychotic children, that I had had to sometimes physically restrain a child by wrapping him up in my arms and legs and sitting on the padded floor while he bashed his head against my chest. I did not want to try this with Eric. I felt it would infuriate him further, and frighten him. He was in a frenzy, and I could think of no context for his distress.

I continued to tolerate Eric's repeated physical attacks and to search for words to say to him. I began to become calmer and less worried. Eric finally exhausted himself. Then he suddenly became very frightened and cowering. It was a profound and rapid transformation; he seemed to have literally collapsed inside. I was able to tell him that I recognized that he was afraid I wanted to "get back at him" for his rages at me. I told him that although I did not know why he was so angry, I wanted to learn, and that I would not hurt him. I was glad this much could be put into words and shared with some clarity. By the end of the session Eric had calmed significantly, as if a storm had passed on through.

Now I think that his outburst signaled the emergence of what might be called the "lost child," that part of Eric's personality frantically seeking a containing mind with alpha function and reverie. I thought my having come through his primal storm was something that began to show him that there could be an actual separate caring other who could survive and begin to think in a time of desperate distress. Bion emphasized that what a child internalizes is not an object, but a link to an object. The quality of the relationship with the object and the object's relationship to the subject both sponsor a shared psychological atmosphere that makes emotional experience tolerable. The absence or presence of alpha function has significant implications for the growth of an "apparatus for thinking." Without this container–contained relationship as a starting point it seems impossible to grow an "apparatus for thinking" and to use it to learn from experience. Though I could not offer Eric a great deal of insight into his storm, I could live through it with him in a live-minded way. I could extend to him my willingness to get to know the storm experience and to bring the energy of the storm into the field of my own embodied attention.

Not long after this session Eric became interested in the sand tray. He selected a small figure of a boy. He did not speak. He took the boy and buried him in the sand. Then he dug him up. Then he buried him again. Then he dug him up and had him walk along the top of the sand, then, suddenly the boy was buried again. This scene had an acute intensity, economy, and emotional condensation. There seemed to be an important story beginning to be told. I asked Eric if there might be any kind of story to go along with what he was showing me. Eric said flatly "No." At this moment I did not seem to appreciate how hard it was for Eric to make stories with words. It was an achievement for him to narrate a story, however rudimentary, through action.

I wondered if the little character he had chosen had a name. "Boy," said Eric. I asked where Boy was. Eric said "In the sand." I said to Eric that as I watched Boy I had a very strong feeling that was hard to put into words. I said the feeling felt like a mixture of worry and fear and sadness all mixed up and confused. At this Eric looked at me and said

"It's a permanent earthquake. It never stops shaking." These words had a striking effect on me. I *felt them* at the level of sensation. It was a kind of turning point for me, a deeper realization of what it might be like to be in Eric's body and to see his picture of the world. I began to wonder inside myself how it could be possible to make a life if that life involves living through a permanent earthquake. At the same time, I felt there was something deeply hopeful about Eric's mind, something very strong in his ability to create such a dramatic personal symbol.

For several weeks I had some pussy willows that a colleague had given me in a vase on the small table near my couch. One day Eric walked up to them and seemed to become lost in curiosity. Silently he reached out and touched one. He said, "It's very hard." I agreed. Then he peeled the shell away and stroked the soft grey bud inside. He said, "It's so soft." Though moved by this I said nothing. He said, "I want to let them all out and set them free," and he began to peel the shells away, leaving the husks on the table while stroking the soft insides. I said to Eric, "I think you are fascinated by discovering the softness of the pussy willows because there is a soft part of you that you wants to be free." I paused. Then I said, "In order to free that soft part you need to know that I will protect it, and you, and not damage it. I know how hard it is to believe that there can be enough protection for you to risk getting to know your soft part of yourself here with me." Eric did not say anything but he gazed for a long time directly into my eyes. Now I recognize how utterly literal such feelings of hardness and softness are for children like Eric. What sounds like a metaphor is in fact a description of an experience as it is felt, somewhere on the border between sensation and image. Words like softness, hardness, and protection describe actual sensual and concrete experiences on the way to becoming true and stable symbols. The emergence of symbols is made possible as the child opens up to becoming rooted in the containing atmosphere of a shared emotional relationship where reverie can be actually felt and realized.

The Emergence of Playing

One day Eric began playing a game with the small fountain in my office. He touched the water gurgling from the spout and felt the smoothness of the flat rocks in the fountain bed. Then he went to the plug in the wall and pulled it out. The water stopped. He put the plug back in the socket and the water resumed flowing. He played this game of in and out, on and off, stopping and starting for several minutes. I said that he was trying to figure out how experiences get interrupted. He said, "I'm invisible." I said he thought I was angry with him for pulling the plug in and out. He said, "You are my brother, the elephant. I'm invisible and you have to find me. I had to leave because the invisible infant 'A' is coming." I wasn't sure I heard him right and he told me again: the "invisible infant 'A' is coming." Then he asked to play with the sand tray and took the sand from the tray and covered the play table with it, making a storm of sand that spread across the floor and onto the furniture. I was not very happy about this mess but I felt it would be wrong to thwart something important that was happening. Eric said that he could come back now because he had a "special detector" that allowed him to know that the "invisible infant A" was now gone. There was nothing silly about this play. There was an atmosphere of suspense, something hard to describe; the words "mysterious" or "solemn" come close. He told me that it was "invisible infant A" who had made the mess with the sand. Perhaps this play with the plug going in and out and connected with the water's flow or its absence can be understood as the emerging capacity for projecting and introjecting. I could imagine that Eric was discovering in his relationship to me an object with a space inside to welcome his projective identifications.

In the sessions that followed, Eric's material became very rich and seemed to spill out with enormous speed and seemingly endless transformations. It was impossible for me to register, reflect upon, and reply to all the variations in his play. He began drawing chaotic explosive messes with black and blue and red and brown crayons. These developed over weeks into mazelike galaxy pictures. One day I decided, spontaneously, to make up a game to help Eric find more words for his drawings. I said, "I have an idea. Let's pretend that you are a scientist (he had given me ample data to know that he imagined himself as a future scientist) and I am a reporter. I am here to report upon these pictures and to learn more about them." Eric said he liked the idea. He told me to get a pad of paper and to take notes. Reporters, he said, have to take notes.

Eric told me about a creature from outer space. He called it a Bloboe. He spelled its name out: "B-l-o-b-o-e." This material is from the report that Eric dictated to me:

> The Bloboe has a fiery mouth; it is very very large; one mouth is always open; there is another mouth that is closed most of the time. The Bloboe is an alien and looks like a rolling pin; it has a very strange mind; its mind is woven together. [I asked by what, but this is not known.] The Bloboe is very strong and has large muscles. It eats lighted matches. The fire burns out when he or she dies. Female bloboes are very rare. Girls have different patterns. They have shorter mouth fire. Their home is in the core of Mars.

The emergence of the messy baby part of himself, and his evocative name "invisible infant A" as well as his attempts to sort out feelings like galaxies and boy and girl confusions marked a watershed in this period of our work. Eric began explicitly wondering about things like "minds," and this development was exciting to both of us. It opened up a new dimension of communication about experiences of separateness and about experiences that can be shared.

The process of becoming rooted now seemed to allow not only more shared attention but the emergence of reciprocal play. One might understand that certain possibilities had emerged because of the new existence of many different kinds of mouths. The open mouth represents sensuousness and the capacity for primary cooperation. The closed mouth represents autosensuousness and the fiery mouth perhaps represents many things, including anticipated pain around taking in, pain around giving and taking, and also a confusing, fiery part-object where the masculine is seen as vastly exaggerated in power in comparison to the feminine.

Discovering a Colony of Souls

One day Eric began his session by wordlessly sorting through the large box of plastic play figures. He selected, for the first time, a small, brightly colored cloth butterfly. He studied the butterfly for a long time, presumably because the intricate pattern of its cloth wings attracted him. Then he looked at me and, still without speaking, got up and made the butterfly move around the room, softly landing on different things—the pillow on the couch, the arm of the chair, the lid of a small ceramic pot. Then he came near me and made the butterfly move around my head and face and ultimately land on the back of my hand. Eric looked at me with an anxious kind of expectancy, as if silently asking "Is this all right?" Then he smiled. I smiled back at him. He told me how happy he was to find the butterfly in the toy box and wondered why I had never put it there before. I said he had never seen it before. He insisted that I had just put it in the toy box today, and I said, no, that I thought it was not the toys that were different, but Eric himself, and in particular the difference was in the sorts of things he was now noticing and also wanting to share with others, including me.

Following this session the butterfly became a regular character in Eric's play for several meetings. In a particularly dramatic sequence, the butterfly was attacked by soldiers who were sent to shoot it. The soldiers, I learned, were at war. They were deaf from so much fighting, and they would not stop until they killed the butterfly. They had no reason to kill the butterfly except that it had accidentally flown into the war. The butterfly, Eric told me, had an invisible language, and no one knew how to translate it. He said that someone had to make a soldier trap to save the butterfly. He then said that some of the soldiers might go on the butterfly's side. He said that if they could build a time machine they could go back to the time when the butterfly could talk. He said that if they did go back in time other soldiers would be waiting when they got there to put them in prison for trying to help the butterfly.

I did not attempt to interpret this material but allowed it to continue to unfold by asking questions and learning as much as I could about the story of the butterfly, the soldiers, the time machine, and other characters that subsequently emerged. I felt that beyond the obviously interesting content of the material, that attention was now being shared in a new way. The feeling of playing and being together, of cooperating and communicating was emerging as Eric narrated this world to me. He included my participation in its evolution, and I felt that holding a space for his exploration of the encounter of beauty, fragility, and cruelty was my most important function.

One of the most interesting developments in Eric's play, some years into our work, was the evolution of an imaginary group called "The Young Animal Society" or the Yaz group. This group included characters like Lion Cub, King Pig, the Gator Brothers, the Little Lamb, the Snake, and several others. The adventures of the Yaz group unfolded over more than a year, and Eric increasingly used these characters to explicitly think about and work through some of his own confusions and concerns.

For example, the earliest members of the Yaz group were the Gator Brothers. These small green plastic alligators both had very large teeth. The Gator Brothers came to represent Eric's impulsive aggressiveness, which he began to work with and think about through the mastery of an imaginary toy called "the chomp machine." The problem for the Gator Brothers was that, before we (Eric and I) invented the chomp machine, they used to chomp on each other. This, not surprisingly, seemed to mirror the behavior between Eric and his little sister, and at a deeper level, perhaps, the undifferentiated predator–prey anxiety that Tustin has so brilliantly described. As the Gator Brothers played out their wildly uncontrollable need to chomp on the always strong enough chomp machine, Eric began to discover a way of thinking about his own impulsiveness in a way that could let him master it. Eventually I could link this back to his explosive session early in our work together.

Many characters evolved through our co-created play world. King Pig, a complex and passionate creature, came to represent the greedy, bossy, have-it-my-way-now part of Eric that he could increasingly recognize, confront, question, and manage. Lion Cub came to represent the grandiose but also ambitious, curious, willing-to-strive aspect of Eric. The Little Lamb represented the small, vulnerable part of himself that was often in danger of falling victim to what Eric ingeniously named "brain-jacking." Brain-jacking is the sensation of fear you feel when you dread being controlled by others. When I took up in the transference Eric's fear of my influence, he assured me that I was not a brain-jacker. He described in compelling ways the evidence that he felt existed for different ways his mother and father, however, used brain-jacking on him. In his play it was the Snake, who, like King Pig, came to represent how intelligence can be captured and exploited by cruel, quasi-malignant states of mind. King Pig and the Snake were the ultimate experts in brain-jacking. Seemingly no one could reform them. They continuously intruded into the sphere of the other animals with greedy, dominating, controlling intentions. But over time the Yaz group as a collective could begin to contain their intrusiveness and protect a communal space (for thinking) where more charitable relationships could develop.

I believe that the therapeutic aspect of this play was in the description and discussion of the life-world of the characters and their actions. Over time, despite many repetitive elements and themes, we could observe together novel moments, thoughts, and solutions to the problems encountered by the different animal members in their communal relations. This activity was a kind of playing and thinking together that was building up capacities that Eric could take from the completely imaginary world of the Yaz group into his own life. I could eventually say things to him like "I think you have a problem just like Lion Cub has today. I think you become frightened of becoming lost on the weekend just as he got lost in the forest without his friends. I think feeling lost makes you feel small and helpless and then, like Lion Cub, you pretend to be a know-it-all in order to make yourself feel better. But that strategy always seems to lead to King Pig arriving and intruding and trying to boss everyone around, and this is what you say your sister was complaining about and that made you so angry." Eric then might say "I'm like King Pig too, aren't I?" We would then try to understand what emotional triggers brought certain Yaz group members into relational conflict. While Eric looked at the members of the Yaz group as dynamic living figures, I looked at them as personifications of states of mind and relationships in evolution and transformation.

It was a relief to see how much pleasure Eric now took in playing. Eric began to consolidate significant self-reflective functions through his play. The complexity and richness of the play sequences indicate, I believe, evidence of the growth of an "apparatus for thinking." Toward the end of our work together, Eric began to make what he called "mind-maps," complicated, mazelike drawings that graphically illustrated some of the problems he felt were in his own mind. He stated that by drawing these mind-maps we could better see what he was feeling and in this way

I could help him more with how to tolerate and work with his concerns.

Evidence of his increased capacity for reflective function translated into his daily life and was confirmed by his mother in one of our last parent meetings. She told me how she had picked Eric up from the Learning Center that he was attending several days a week. She told him that they could not go straight home, as he would have expected, because she needed to run an urgent errand first. She told me she could see how angry this made Eric because he clenched his jaw and his fists and turned away from her to stare out the window. She was able to say to him that she thought he was very upset about not being able to go home right away but that it would only be a few extra minutes. She said that Eric had turned back to her and said "You're right, Mom. I'd like to kill you right now. But I'll get over it." Carol, to her credit, had learned over the years not to take Eric's words so concretely and was able to appreciate now how new it was for him to speak to her directly about the intensity of his feelings, rather than acting them out. In this way, though the feeling was still intense, she could share more of Eric's experience, and Eric could gradually begin to picture her experience in ways he had never before been able to.

The Fate of Attention

Eric's treatment can be understood within the larger context of the theme of attention. Attention is a complex phenomenon. It is generally understood as a capacity having varying qualities that allows one to focus on important aspects of the environment. From a psychoanalytic point of view, Meltzer, following Freud, has highlighted the importance of being able to direct attention inward. Meltzer (1992) says that "attention is the tiller by which we steer the organ of consciousness about in the teeming world of psychic qualities" (p. 29). Similarly, as Stern and his colleagues (1998) write, "Now moments are not part of the set of characteristic present moments that make up the usual way of being together and moving along. They demand an intensified attention and some kind of choice" (p. 911). Taking Meltzer and Stern together, we can begin to imagine the question of the "fate of attention." Can one direct attention inwardly? When one does, what kinds of internal objects capture one's attention? How is attention deployed in a free and creative way? What is the role of the actual external other in capturing or freeing attention in a moment of emotional contact? Tustin's descriptions of the use of attention give us important clues to explore and describe the fate of attention.

The fate of attention, it seems, is organized very early in what might be called forms of proto-attention. How attention as a capacity develops is deeply linked to what Tustin has described as "primary sensuousness." Tustin (1992) writes:

> Psychotherapeutic work with autistic states in children indicates that the flux of sensations which constitute the infant's primary sense of being has two main head-streams. There is *sensuousness*, which is directed towards the body of other human beings who are experienced as responsive and alive; and there is *auto-sensuousness*, which is directed towards the subject's own body, or parts of other bodies experienced as if they were parts of the subject's body.... infant observation suggests that in normal development, from the beginning of life, *consciousness* [my italics] of the very young infant flits, in a flexible way, between these two states. But trouble is in store if auto-sensuousness becomes over-reactive and over-developed. Such abnormal over-reactive auto-sensuous developments mean that primary sensuousness is *distracted away from becoming focused on succouring, nuturant figures* [my italics], and thus from developing relationships with them. (p. 28)

Attention, and therefore consciousness, is organized and deployed according to sensuous and auto-sensuous trends. Drawing on Tustin's formulation of the differences between sensuousness and auto-sensuousness, I suggest that Eric experienced differing qualities of what I shall call now-here experiences. I differentiate a now-here experience from Stern's "now moment." My intent in doing so is to imagine the primal organization of attention, through Tustin's categories of primary sensuousness and auto-sensuousness, that later leads to what Stern has named present moments, moving along, and now moments.

Primary sensuousness and auto-sensuousness represent two quite different forms of now-here experience. It is not the absence of attention we must be concerned with, but the form that attention takes and the use to which it is being put. It is especially essential that the therapist differentiate and describe these two different forms of now-here focus that are primary or rudimentary in undertaking the task of observing autistic states and behaviors.

Primary sensuousness, according to Tustin, is a relational experience that sponsors the development of primary cooperation. The model for primary cooperation is the good-enough feed between mother and infant. In this scenario, the child's capacity to be now-here involves an emotional experience shared with an actual external other. Notably, this passionate relationship is characterized by the capacity to share attention. Tustin (1986) has written beautifully about the importance of the early suckling experience. She observes:

> This is where relationship begins. Clinical work indicates that the *sensation* of the nipple-in-mouth (or teat of the bottle experienced in terms of an inbuilt gestalt of the breast) is the focus for the development of the psyche. Associated with the mother's encircling arms, her shining eyes, and *the mutual concentration of their attention* [my italics], it becomes the core of the self. It becomes associated with regulation, with bearing the suspense of waiting, with tolerating human limitations, with boundaries and with the sorting out of sensations. The way in which the 'breast' is given and the way in which it is taken leaves a mark for good or ill on the developing psyche. This will be affected by the child's responses and by the quality of the mother's relationship to the infant's father, and by the circumstances of the parent's own infancy.
>
> In normal development, the heightened degree of responsiveness and the *especial quality of attention* [my italics] of both the suckling mother and her infant partake of the sublime, and even of the 'mystical'. It is a physically based psychic experience. This empathic communion is the earliest form of communication. It fosters the growth of the psyche. (p. 29)

In contrast, when it is decoupled from experiences of primary sensuousness, auto-sensuousness generates ever more isolating and idiosyncratic now-here experience. In an auto-sensuous scenario, attention is used to create autistic shapes and objects that block out awareness of the not-me world, or to entangle and confuse the developing self with the other. In Stern's view this use of auto-sensuousness would block out the experience of shared present moments, the experience of moving along, and the discovery of deep connection in now moments.

Tustin (1986) writes:

> It is important to realize that, since the child's body seems fused with 'autistic objects', these have scarcely reached the status of an 'object' in the usual sense of the term. The child's *attention* becomes so riveted upon these hard, object-like clusters of sensations that they prevent the normal use of actual objects, distinguished as objects which are separate from the body. They also prevent the development of relationships with people, who—by contrast with autistic objects, which are always available—seem unreliable. (p. 128, my italics)

When primary cooperation and communication are established in the first days and weeks of infancy, a "background presence of primary identification" (Grotstein) allows for a flexible and mobile form of attention to evolve. This proto-attention, as Tustin says, shifts back and forth between self-sensation and exploration of the other. The premature awareness of two-ness, as may have occurred in Eric's case, can create a traumatic hole or wound, and in such situations the proto-attention of the infant can be swept up in the creation of barrier-type defenses linked to omnipotence as a survival function (Symington, 1985). The fate of attention in this scenario may evolve into overreliance on such defenses as adhesive equation and adhesive identification, as well as the development of the pseudo-object relations so cogently described by Mitrani (1996).

I believe that Eric's capacity to share attention must have been obstructed in the earliest weeks and months of his life. Tustin described the use of attention to create autistic shapes and objects through the manipulation of sensations. Such a process creates a form of rigid, captured attention that is used as a barrier to the awareness of the not-me world or to entangle the self with the other. While Eric's functioning was not completely dominated by auto-sensuous phenomena, he seemed to be a boy who struggled terribly with being unrooted and who repeatedly turned toward entangling auto-sensuousness as a mode of coping with what he perceived to be the threat of unbearable experience. The disability of Eric's attention system contributed the development of idiosyncratic modes of behaving—miscarriages of motivation in Tustin's language—put in place as ways of trying to organize and manage his increasingly difficult-to-regulate experience.

Through our work together, Eric gradually began to discover the capacity to reclaim attention and to develop shared attention. I'm suggesting that Eric began to differentiate two kinds of now-here experience. Auto-sensuous now-here experience does not allow for shared experience, while the experience of sensuous, shared, now-here experience evolves into what Stern has called "moments of meeting" because it involves the discovery of reliable containing relationships.

Eric's capacity to share experience and use my mind gradually helped him to establish a "humanizing process" and to evolve a viable apparatus for thinking. The achievement of shared attention then allowed for the discovery and transformation of emotional experience. Such shared attention is a vital element at the heart of Tustin's notion of the therapeutic action of psychotherapy. Tustin (1992) writes:

> As the child begins to feel held in our awareness by our thought, care, and concern for him, he begins to hold experiences in his own mind as thoughts, memories, and imaginations. The undue use of autistic objects begins to wane. As Dr. Bion has pointed out, the mother mediates sanity to the nursling as well as nourishing milk. By their sensible attention and behavior, therapists can convey such sanity also. The feeling-tone of the therapeutic session is of especial importance to the psychotic child. (p. 123)

I would like to make clear that the now-here experiences of attention that I am seeking to differentiate are not transitional experiences as described by Winnicott. The discovery of transitional space, according to Winnicott, is linked to creativity, spontaneity, and to the freedom to explore experiences of emotional intensity against a background of supportive illusion (Winnicott, 1990). In transitional space, subject and object are neither acknowledged as separate nor fused and confused. They occupy an intermediate space, a space Winnicott called a paradox. The subjective experience of transitional relating has a distinct quality and texture as well as an atmosphere of play and shared attention. The now-here states that I am now interested in describing constitute the preconditions for play (primary cooperation) or else profound obstructions to play and transitional relating (isolating auto-sensuousness).

Another important domain of now-here experience that I do not explore in this essay involves the complex phenomenology of the geography of fantasy and confusions of life space, as described by Meltzer (1975). Intrusive identification is an important phenomenon that is beyond the scope of this communication, although it certainly is of interest with regard to the theme of "brain-jacking" that emerged in Eric's play.

Finally, this case material demonstrates, I believe, an important and under-recognized element in Tustin's insight into the development of the mind: the importance of attention and its early roots. The work of describing different forms of experience generated by differing uses of attention allows the analyst to better appreciate and even imaginatively enter the child's world in order to lend words to the textures and qualities of isolating experiences. Gradually, through expanding observation as well as deepening reverie, the fortunate analyst may be able to help woo the child into contact with the transformational possibilities of a shared attention, one that expands tolerance for play, surprise, and psychic evolution.

As Tustin (1992) has written, "Fortunately, there is always a part of the child, however minuscule, which wants to grow up properly and can listen to us and use our words for the purposes of growth, and for freedom from the rigidity and artificiality of his autistic encumbrances" (p. 166).

CHAPTER FIVE

From Nowhere to Now-Here:
Reflections on Buddhism and Psychotherapy

 Anything looked at with love and attention becomes very interesting.

— Gary Snyder

UDDHA WAS A MAN WHO BECAME AWAKENED TO what are described as the Four Noble Truths, the underlying laws of experience and reality. To accomplish his awakening, Buddha took his own mind and experience as the basic objects of investigation. The deeper he penetrated into the causes and conditions of suffering, generated by the habits of his mind and by his conditioned perceptions, the more freedom he experienced emotionally. This freedom opened into a vast view of human experience characterized by a great compassion for the suffering of all sentient beings.

Buddhism begins with the recognition that suffering is real. Suffering touches every life in some form with some intensity. This is a difficult recognition to accept although the evidence for it is everywhere. The truth of suffering is intimidating. We are often so ill-prepared to face suffering directly that we create "nowhere" states of mind to dull our mental pain. Alienated nowhere states of mind help evade the now-here experience of painful emotional reality, including the ubiquity of psychic and physical violence.

Buddha taught that the causes of suffering can be investigated. These causes can be identified in each of our lives. Investigating the causes of suffering requires courage, compassion, and sustained commitment. Meditation is one of the main tools used to prepare the mind for such a task.

Once the causes of suffering have been learned about, Buddha taught that one can decrease, even bring to an end, the unskillful habits of mind that give rise to and perpetuate suffering. By discovering the ways that we create and prolong suffering in others, and ourselves, we can gradually deconstruct the styles of suffering woven into character and identity.

I have been studying Buddhism since 1991, seriously practicing daily meditation since 1995. I have been influenced by many Buddhist teachers, but my primary inspiration comes from H. H. Dalai Lama, the lineage of H. H. Dudjom Rinpoche, and the kindness of my teacher Lama Yeshe Wangmo. My interest in Buddhism is very personal, not academic. I want to emphasize this point at the beginning. For me, Buddhist practice brings into the foreground the central importance of the fate of attention in daily living. My teachers have instructed me to concentrate on actual practice and meditation. They assert that, in the long run, practical experience in mindfully investigating the fate of attention is much more important than intellectual knowledge. This emphasis has become increasingly helpful to me. I endeavor to remember to continuously return my attention to the details, textures, and shapes of my own constantly arising experience.

I have also trained to be a psychoanalyst working with children and adults. My training had a particular focus in British Object Relations, especially the pioneering work of the English psychoanalysts Melanie Klein, Wilfred Bion, and Donald Winnicott. Sigmund Freud discovered the lasting emotional influence of the child within the adult. Melanie Klein, and those who followed her, exposed the central importance of the experiences of the very first weeks and months of the infant's life. Our earliest emotional experiences, Klein asserts, exert a lifelong influence on the developing structure of the mind through the experiences of unconscious phantasy. For Klein, it is the fate of anxiety that matters most in how we come to perceive the world and ourselves.

Contemporary psychoanalysis, like Buddhism, investigates the complex conditions that generate and influence subjective experience. In our perceptions of ourselves and of others, and in our views of what is possible in personal and group relationships, there is an important link between anxiety and attention that I will begin to describe in this chapter. Psychoanalysis creates the special conditions that make possible an intimate interpersonal investigation of the ways our choices are shaped, mostly unconsciously, by our reactions to and means of coping with varying degrees of emotional pain and anxiety. Developing the capacity to bring compassionate attention to the experience of anxiety and mental pain is a task shared in different ways by both Buddhism and psychoanalysis. What follows, then, are several short sketches of experience, informed by both Buddhist and psychoanalytic points of view, loosely held together by the themes and variations of pain and attention.

Knowing

Human beings are emotional creatures. Faced with the ordinary complexity of daily life that often generates frustration, uncertainty, anxiety, fear, anger, and even feelings of helplessness, we unconsciously seek, as small children naturally do, the safety and refuge of an apparently all-knowing (parental) figure. The wish to be with someone who knows defends, if imperfectly, against the terrors of uncertainty. The need to know is, at a deep unconscious level, equated with survival. Not-knowing is equated with doom.

The idea of the unconscious as a powerful influence in the way we live out our lives has become trivialized in popular culture today. What Freud asserted, in fact, remains both deeply relevant and troubling. Freud's vision of the human subject is that of a person unknowingly trapped between past and future, unable to inhabit the present moment, always somehow incompletely aware. In Freud's scheme, desire and reality clash at the intersection of personal experience. The experience of "I" is constellated in this perpetual collision and must mediate between impersonal instincts seeking satisfaction, the demands of the family and the larger group, the processes of dreaming and wish fulfillment, and the accidents and existential variables introduced by the contexts of daily life. In Freud's sobering view of human life, we can not only never completely master the external environment with our will to know, but we are also faced with the reality of an internal world, a psychical emotional environment created by a lifetime of experience that is largely unexplored and always at least partially unknown to us.

What makes it so difficult for us to know ourselves and others more completely? Freud answered that almost any object can be invested with some form of what he named transference. We transfer both our desires and their frustrations from childhood relationships and modes of being into the emotional experiences of our adult lives. It is not just that too much detail, information, or emotion are present for us to cope with, moment to moment, but that transference clouds our relationship to the now-here heart of experience with the thick shadows of the past. The subjective benefit of this transference process is the illusion of certainty and familiarity that it sponsors. The cost of this habit of mind is that we repeatedly alienate ourselves, sometimes profoundly, from some smaller or larger part of our now-here experience.

The analytic experience is a learning process. The psychoanalyst creates the conditions to investigate both how we learn, emotionally, and how we fail to learn from our experience. She does this by inviting the patient to enter into a special kind of intimate conversation. To facilitate this special conversation the analyst requests that the patient agree to regular, frequent meetings, sometimes three, four, or five times per week. These meetings occur in the same place, at the same time, and for the same fixed duration. The analyst's office is often more like a comfortable room in a home than a sterile doctor's office. The patient may choose to recline on a couch with the analyst seated behind or he may choose to sit in a comfortable chair, facing the analyst. Reclining on the couch has the benefit of allowing the patient to experience his own spontaneous inner wanderings, anxieties, and image-life. The purpose of this carefully constructed and protected setting is to promote an emotional atmosphere of openness and to encourage the possibilities for expression.

In the initial sessions, the instruction is given that the patient should say whatever comes to mind. After that, the sessions are left radically open. Often people find this invitation to openness much more nerve-racking than they might have anticipated. It is, of course, a slightly bizarre situation, one, I think, of radical generosity when compared to many other conventional settings of everyday life. A patient's first attempts at free association are often frustrating. There is an obvious parallel to the person beginning to experiment with meditation. We are often surprised by our own mental worlds and frustrated that our capacity to attend to ourselves is so underdeveloped. Much patience is needed to begin both these kinds of explorations. Endurance is a valued quality that grows with patience.

The British psychoanalyst Wilfred Bion once wrote that when two individuals meet, an emotional storm is created. The patient often crosses the threshold of the analyst's doorstep bringing a storm with him. When we stop to look at the life of the mind, whether in solitary meditation or in the analytic conversation, we find a simple truth: our minds are often very stormy! Many patients come seeking shelter or refuge from the storm's intensifying force. Over time the storm gathers in the consulting room and, although he may fear its emergence and intensity, the patient experiences the darkly gathered clouds parting, session after session. From this sometimes long period of testing each other, the patient and analyst may experience an emerging new space, one where both individuals share the risk of surrendering to the opportunity of free association and creative exploration. Rather than be the knower, a temptation she must eschew, the analyst becomes an observer and describer. Optimally, the patient comes to share this task. Each individual participates in observing in his or her own unique way the development of a shared emotional relationship that becomes both trusted and deeply valued over time.

Psychoanalysis is not meditation, but it may aspire to a similar level of attention. As sessions unfold, storms are not the only things that arise. Bits of dreams arise. Currents of memory trickle forth. There is a tale of hatred to be told, a story of desire to be felt, a realization of ignorance to face. The poignancy of sadness and regret gradually emerges. The entire Buddhist Wheel of Life may be partially glimpsed. Demons and gods and hungry ghosts trouble the conversation. Grasping, aversion, delusion, and the energy of perpetual wishing unfold to view. All of the 10,000 things seem to exist not only outside but inside. Sometimes the session has the atmosphere of a dream, sometimes the vivid concreteness of a nightmare. Throughout it all, the task shared by both analyst and patient is to observe experience, to lend words to emotions, and to bring attention to that which may never before have been lovingly attended to.

I sought psychoanalysis with a powerful, semiconscious wish to become some kind of expert, to become someone who *knows*. People often seek a similar intense sense of knowing from the guru, and hope that

Buddhism will be a direct path to omniscience. Instead of becoming the Knower, redeemed by omniscience, psychoanalysis gave me the opportunity to discover myself in emotional ways I could not have achieved on my own. My analyst helped me to begin to become familiar with rage, shame, fear, and intense anxieties I had never been encouraged to know about earlier. This meant learning to identify, tolerate, and work directly with the many ways my own emotional experience had not yet become part of my own self-reflective history. My past experiences had remained so alive they continuously intruded into the present, shaping my future in many unintended ways.

Psychoanalysis, in my view, seeks to sponsor a realization of mental freedom that grows into an attitude of resilient openness toward experience. For a long time, the "I" engaged in analysis must tolerate being riddled with questions. One basic and perplexing question that arises is the location of experience in relation to the categories past, present, and future. Contrary to popular images of psychoanalysis as interminably digging up the past, what analysis investigates is the immense difficulty we all seem to have of living consciously in the present moment. In my view, the task of psychoanalysis is to reclaim the future, particularly from the intrusive hegemony of our unconscious transferences and our unintentional repetitions of the disowned pain of the past.

Hate

The symbolism of the Tibetan Wheel of Life is beautiful. The Wheel of Life symbolizes the nature and causes of cyclic existence. Three figures at the very center of the wheel represent what are called the three poisons: hatred, possessiveness, and ignorance. Hatred, pictured as a snake, symbolizes one of the main obstacles to healing and liberation. In order to heal, difficult realities like hate must be faced. The examination of hate makes possible the lessening of the ways that we unconsciously perpetuate such poisons and their consequences through our thoughts and fantasies, interpersonal speech, and concrete actions. Hate is a pervasive and powerful state of mind. It is a state that is often enacted, rather than acknowledged. I seek to lend words to the experience.

What does hate feel like? Some people hate their parents, some their lovers. Some people hate their children, some the circumstances of their birth or class. People hate differences that they endow with toxic significance. People hate ideas or they hate feelings. Some people hate particular emotions, like intense sadness. Hatred of powerlessness, helplessness, and vulnerability are common and understandable. Some people hate time and its passing. Other people hate death or sickness or old age. Hatred, it seems, always has an object. It is frightening indeed to meet someone who simply hates, without an object to focus this energy. Hate, then, is commonplace. People dip into hate, and reemerge. But some people swim in hate the way fish swim in water.

I think there is a difference between ordinary hate and malignant hate. Melanie Klein spoke about the splitting of the self and the object in order to preserve feelings of goodness and wholeness and to disown experiences of distress and fragmentation. Normal hate gets worked through as one of many kinds of emotional experience a person can gradually learn to transform, especially with the caring help of others. Malignant hate is something else. People can become totally identified with the power of destructive hating. People can come to depend upon hate for an illusion of invincibility and belonging. Hate organizes their egos and even, bizarrely, makes them feel safer. Sometimes hatred traps aliveness within it and acts as a wall against collapse into terrible deadness and despair. The world becomes upside down. Hate is good and peacemaking bad, a sign of weakness and a lack of resolve.

The result of chronic and intense experiences of frustration and pain and the repeated failure to interpersonally transform distress into comfort leads individuals to feel intense toxic shame. Toxic shame is ego-destructive rather than constructive and the root of many of the phenomena characteristic of hating. Toxic shame involves the chronic feeling of threat to the psychophysical survival of the self. One schizophrenic patient told me, "I have no mandate for life." For patients living with an internal atmosphere of toxic, ego-destructive shame, even the smallest details of daily life can become distorted evidence of obstructive intentions on the part of others or even of the world itself. Saturated by experiences of toxic shame, one feels oneself to be the passive object of an active hatred. The hatred of emotion may become the hatred of all experience and may at last grow so large that the person feels that living itself is equated with the experience of hating and being hated.

Malignant hatred poses serious immediate risks. People can be so immersed in their distorted perceptions that they will kill without apparent conflict. I remember a former gang member I once worked with briefly. As a young teen he had witnessed a murder in his neighborhood, and it had deeply frightened him. As a young man he became a murderer himself. He hated the person he killed, and at the same time knew almost nothing about the person. He rationalized his premeditated attack as self-defense. When he came out of prison, he began to change because he became a father. Somehow, being in the protective role of a parent to his new baby son made him reconsider his commitment to violence as a value system.

Several angry men have described to me how hate functions according to rules of intensity and amplification. Hate smolders until some detail triggers it. Hate and shame seem to go together. The awful intensity of shame requires some kind of container. Hate serves as a kind of second skin, or armor. The irony is that the surface of violence, belligerence, and ruthless provocation only engages more hating reactions from the surrounding world. The mental pain such men feel is often aggressively evacuated through violent speech or violent action. Hating can intoxicate. People become addicted to hating.

Hatred also numbs the capacity to think. People have described the literal narrowing and darkening of vision in states of hate, as if one were entering a tunnel. I have experienced this too when overwhelmingly angry, but it was a transient feeling. One can go dead to hate, or be swept up in its swirling energy. When inundated with feelings of shame and hate, people seek any relief they can find. Some groups provide an organized discourse of hate. The experience of hate groups seems to be like going inside a special world, sponsoring the vivid perception that all that feels toxic can be displaced and located outside. The logic of purity and decay, involving splitting, idealization, and denigration, organizes such groups. It is possible to live inside hate itself.

Hate, then, can become woven into one's identity. Beneath hate for others lies the terror of the self being destroyed. People who hate malignantly idealize the protective force of hate but unconsciously don't believe that protection can be real. Hate serves as a kind of thin insulation from the terror of all that can never be controlled. Hate fills the space where love should be. Hate fills the space where terror was, and organizes a world that is too chaotic, too unpredictable, and too uncontrollable. Some children are unfortunate enough to find people who help them to cultivate their hate. They have coaches in hating and violent perception. Their attention becomes captured by hate. Hate creates a fascination that can be used for brainwashing. Hate exploits evidence of real problems that need solution and fuels destructive reactions against the pain of so much unfinished work.

Freud's and Klein's approaches to hate have been developed by Bion in a direction that bridges biological, intrapsychic, and interpersonal dimensions. Bion described what he called an *obstructive object relationship.* He felt that some patients with catastrophically vulnerable backgrounds come to anticipate that almost everyone they contact will inevitably be rejecting of their needs. Bion asserts that a phenomenology of violent rejection suggests a background of catastrophe that the person lives within and unconsciously perpetuates as part of the legacy of early traumatic experiences. Practically speaking, an obstructive object is experienced as someone or something actively hostile toward emotional experience. Rejection generates hatred. People experiencing such obstruction inhabit pervasive states of mind that Buddhists symbolize as the energies of the hell realms populated by hell beings and the hungry ghosts.

Cultivating Not-Knowing and Getting-to-Know

After some years of analysis, I had almost talked myself into the idea that my projections had at least diminished if not more or less ceased to obstruct my perceptions. I remember having this naive view corrected when I visited my Buddhist teacher. I had asked to see her for advice about my meditation practice. As we sat face to face on the floor, she asked me why I had requested the meeting and I was suddenly helplessly tongue-tied. When I started to speak all that came out was gibberish. I felt like I was cracking up. She did not immediately rescue me from this mounting discomfort. She sat quietly, relaxed, meeting my gaze, and finally asked me, gently, to describe my daily practice. Doing so, grounded me and I was able to complete the interview.

Now, I can wonder why I had this powerful reaction to my teacher. I think I transferred my desire to know from analysis to Buddhism and made my Buddhist teacher an even more idealized figure than my analyst. My analyst helped me to become open enough to allow others to teach me. He helped me to face my terror of dependence and my belief that depending on others can only bring catastrophe. My Buddhist teachers have helped me to work with another dimension of idealizing and transference. They have shown me that what my mind generates is nothing to be intimidated by. It is as thin or as thick as I make it. Ultimately, they say, I will realize my thoughts are empty. They are no more or less real than a dream.

My teachers encourage me to repeatedly question the concreteness of my experience. They continuously remind me to simply become aware of what I am feeling, thinking, and doing in the moment. This kind of repeated reclaiming of attention is, they argue, the only practice I need to deepen and perfect in order to dwell in the now-here vividness of reality.

In a similar way, Bion advised the analyst, when entering each session, to eschew memory, desire, and understanding. This advice is commonly misinterpreted to mean that the analyst should try to make his or her mind a blank slate. Anyone who has ever tried meditation knows what frustration follows from such an intention. What Bion encouraged was not to attempt to become an empty consciousness, but rather to bracket those thoughts that focus on what the analyst thinks he already knows (memory), what he hopes to know (desire), and what he intends to interpret (understanding). In recognizing these categories of intention, and in learning to let them fall away into the background of consciousness, Bion felt the analyst had a better chance to become more receptive, more capable of being surprised by new evolutions of experience as they arise within a session. Bion, following and reviving Freud's advice to listen with free-floating attention was, I believe, trying to define and expand the conditions that would allow the analyst to better learn to listen to himself listening to the patient.

The deeper purpose of this task, as it is in Buddhism, is to realize a choiceless attention capable of recognizing and dwelling in spontaneous presence, in the suchness of the emergent moment. The realization of spontaneous presence eludes description. Such experiences open the possibility of perceiving a basic goodness that exists and can be recognized amid the realities of violence, death, and horror. Our task is to learn to dwell in this awareness as a "background presence of primary identification" (Grotstein). Bion emphasized the need to repeatedly open up to a process of getting-to-know. Willingness to explore, to continuously risk the turbulence of turning toward the new, is everything.

The Necessity of Compassion

Something Buddhism describes that analysis, I think, insufficiently considers, is how much compassion is needed to proceed down this path of getting-to-know. In Buddhism, one explicitly practices developing compassion for the hard task of learning to be more open to painful emotional experience.

There is nothing theoretical or sticky sweet about real compassion. Bringing compassion to pain helps. The Buddhist teacher Stephen Levine gives the following example. Imagine you are pounding a nail and you accidentally hit your finger. What is your first response? It is probably not an instant recognition that at this very moment you would benefit from a sense of calm, patient, loving kindness in order to care for your injury. Levine's point is obvious. We meet pain with aversion and with harsh condemnation. When people feel vulnerable they harden their hearts against exposure to pain. We expect rejection, intrusion, denigration, and shame as the order of things. So we hide our pain. We all know this attitude of hatred toward what can be intense and shocking pain. Hatred seems to be part of having a mind that registers pain.

Levine (1989) speaks of moving beyond the ownership of pain (my pain, your pain) through investigating the experience of "the pain." Pain is a given, he says. Suffering can be thought of as our habitually unskillful reactions to pain. Suffering equals pain multiplied by our resistance to pain (Young, 1997). Compassion, in this context, is common sense. Why amplify your pain by fighting it and condemning it? Why not learn how to soften to pain? Why not learn to offer kindly attention to pain? Why not begin to investigate pain? To learn its shape, its texture, its rising and ebbing intensities, its shifting locations, its sticking and melting points? To train the mind to do this would be to create the conditions for

Suffering = pain x resistance to pain (Young)

the transformation of pain, from moment to moment.

In this context, I recall an experience with my analyst. I was very angry and I had the feeling he didn't appreciate the depth of my anger. I was in a great deal of mental pain and it seemed to just keep growing and amplifying. Finally, I told him that the only way I could get my point across would be to buy a gun, bring it to my next session, and fill him full of bullets. This outburst frightened me. I had the feeling I was halfway stuck in a nightmare. His reply was direct, clear, and clarifying. It even had a note of humor. Had he reacted with violent aversion to my pain, our work might have faltered badly. It takes a great deal of trust to risk being honest with others and ourselves about the intensities generated by pain. My analyst's compassion contained the pain and helped to deepen our work. It sponsored a feeling of sincere gratitude and new possibilities for strengths of mind I had never really imagined, much less realized.

Pema Chodron (1997), a nun in the Tibetan Buddhist tradition, writes:

> To stay with the shakiness—to stay with a broken heart, with a rumbling stomach, with the feeling of hopelessness and wanting to get revenge—that is the path of true awakening. Sticking with the uncertainty, getting the knack for relaxing in the midst of chaos, learning not to panic—this is the spiritual path. Getting the knack for catching ourselves, of gently and compassionately catching ourselves, is the path of a warrior. We catch ourselves one zillion times as once again, whether we like it or not, we harden into resentment, bitterness, righteous indignation—harden in any way, even into a sense of relief, a sense of inspiration.... Every day, at the moment when things get edgy, we can ask ourselves, "Am I going to practice peace, or am I going to practice war?" (pp. 10–11)

The Fate of Attention

Attention to the topic of attention has seemed sparse in my analytic training. This is odd, because the fate of attention has an important place in psychoanalysis. It was of particular concern to Freud, Sullivan, and Bion, to name a few. Paying attention to attention is, for me, at the heart of what it means to be a psychoanalyst and to work psychoanalytically.

The late British psychoanalyst Nina Coltart, also a Buddhist, has written:

> It is in the early stages of learning to be analysts and therapists when we are developing our technique, our confidence and our clinical acumen...that the use of 'bare attention' absolutely has to be the scaffolding of everything else we do. Even when we are doing nothing (or appear to be), sitting in silence, testing our faith in the process—our constant, perhaps I should say our only attitude is one of 'bare attention'. In this we try to teach ourselves so continuously to observe, and watch, and listen, and feel, in silence, that this kind of attention becomes—in the end—second nature. It is the bedrock of the day's work. And it is as this bedrock that it becomes forgotten and overlooked. (1992, p. 181)

What do I mean by attention? There is nothing mysterious or mystical about attention. We are all familiar with it. We pay attention in many different ways to many different things throughout an ordinary day. Indeed, unless we are significantly impaired in some way, we are so familiar with attention that we fail to notice how much a part of ordinary perception attention really is.

Greenberg and Snell (1999), quoting Robert Sylwester, define the tasks of attention:

> [A] well-functioning attentional system must fulfill several tasks, including identification of important elements in the environment, the ability to ignore irrelevant stimuli while sustaining attention to the primary focus, the ability to access inactive memories, and the capacity to shift attention rapidly as the result of new information. (p. 108)

Buddhism explicitly advises us to pay attention to attention. Meditation is the vehicle for experimenting with attention. By learning to develop skills of attention, we can investigate the various habits of perception that shape our sense of self and other. Over time, we become familiar with the constantly changing fate of our attention. Rob Nairn (1999), an instructor in the Tibetan Kagyu tradition, writes that "in meditation, we are not working with the success/failure paradigm at all. We are simply training ourselves to be present in the moment with exactly what is there. For most people the big surprise is that what is there is a bewildering stranger" (p. 4).

I once kept a meditation journal. A few excerpts may briefly illustrate how meditation helps one practice paying attention to attention.

April
I bring my attention gently to my breath, to the sensation of the breath entering my nose and leaving. My breath is shallow. I tell myself to let go of my tension. I feel there are layers upon layers of tension blocking relaxation. I begin to concentrate more, to "gather in" my scattered attention, to focus only on my breath, according to my teacher's instructions. Quickly, however, my mind begins to stray. I note "wandering" or "worrying," "planning," "anger," "have to do this right." I feel, as I often do, a concentration of anxious tension in my lower middle back. This time, however, I do not allow it to take over my attention. I don't try to shake it off. Just to observe it. I note "tension, middle back" and move on. My mind wanders again. I pull back the focus to my breath.

July
There is a prideful mind. A mind that says, "I'm doing this right" and "I'm going to be better for it." I try to meet these feelings with attention and loving kindness. I try neither to judge them nor to make them go away. There is an angry mind. "I'm not feeling well, I don't have the energy for this." I try to meet this mind with attention and loving kindness. There is a helpless mind, a mind that desires to be taken care of, like a baby, rocked to sleep. I try to meet this mind with loving kindness. There is a rushing mind, an intellectual mind. There is an aggressive mind, an im-

patient mind. There is a desiring mind, the grasping mind. There is, most of all, a controlling mind. I try to meet all these attitudes with attention and loving kindness.

September

The moment, this instant, can feel so expansive. The moment seems to open up. To just be here, now, my bare feet on the wood floor, the bitter taste of this morning's cup of coffee still in my mouth. I hear the fan in the background and the sound of a seaplane's engine as it descends. I look out at the treetops and deep blue sky. Francisco Varela says somewhere that we teach our children to read and write and do arithmetic but we do not teach them the skills to play the instrument of their own being.

As you become familiar with the practice of meditation, you can see and feel that there are different qualities of attention. Attention can be focused, or dispersed. It can be split and divided. It can be alternating or fixed. It can be full or depleted. One can also speak of the objects of attention. Attention can be directed to both material and immaterial objects. Consider this passage from William James's *The Principles of Psychology* (1890):

When we take a general view of the wonderful stream of our consciousness, what strikes us first is the different pace of its parts. Like a bird's life, it seems to be an alternation of flights and perchings. The rhythm of language expresses this, where every thought is expressed in a sentence and every sentence is closed by a period. The resting-places are usually occupied by sensorial imaginations, whose peculiarity is that they can be held before the mind for an indefinite time, and contemplated without changing; the places of flight are filled with thoughts of relations, static or dynamic, that for the most part obtain between the matters contemplated in the periods of comparative rest. (pp. 115–16)

James has a keen grasp of inner experience and through his power of observation he shows how saturated mental experience can be. He suggests that the structure of language itself creates the possibility of a space between two thoughts. However, that space is immediately unconsciously filled by "sensorial imaginations" that capture attention. The Buddhist student immediately recognizes this description. The goal for meditation is to allow the mind to become quiet, so quiet that one can recognize the emptiness (the opportunity) of a space between two thoughts. It is in this space between that we can fleetingly recognize the nature of awareness itself. Thoughts are immaterial objects that so easily capture our attention that we may even find our attention held hostage by them. Indeed, so much of our attention seems habitually captured by thinking that we may become alienated from more basic bodily experiences: what it feels like to sit, to breath, to chew, to notice the reliability of our own heart's beating. Where was the thought the moment before it arises?

Captured Attention

We are all familiar at some level with the way attention can become captured by an object, whether that object is an emotion, a sensation, an image, a thought (or train of thoughts) or a wish. Attention can be captured by pleasure or pain. Desire captures attention until satisfaction arrives. The pain of yearning is bittersweet compared to the pain of raw frustration. Intense pain, whether mental or physical, tends to capture attention and give rise to the phenomenon Buddhists call aversion. Freud wrote about this very early in his work. In his 1911 paper "Formulations Regarding the Two Principles in Mental Functioning," he notes that, "We have long observed that every neurosis has the result, and therefore probably the purpose, of forcing the patient out of real life, of alienating him from actuality" (p. 13). He continues:

The neurotic turns away from reality because he finds it unbearable—either whole or parts of it. The most extreme type of this alienation from reality is shown in certain cases of hallucinatory psychosis, which aim at denying the existence of the particular event that occasioned the outbreak of insanity. But actually every neurotic does the same with some fragment of reality. (p. 13)

The need to control awareness of what painfully impinges upon us begins at birth, if not before. The means an infant has for filtering painful sensory experiences are at first quite limited. Since infants cannot think about or reflect upon their experiences and are highly limited in their ability to sooth themselves physically, they must rely upon the care and mediating attention of others. Often, the infant's own nascent attention is split between pain and pleasure and is pressed into service *as a defense against distress.* The tradition of infant observation in England, pioneered by Esther Bick and John Bowlby, has produced many detailed descriptions of the role of attention, particularly captured attention, in responding to pain even in the newborn's earliest experiences. In this chapter there is space only to point toward how important this phenomenon of attention's fate can be, both clinically and from a developmental point of view.

The development of the attentional system in infancy unfolds interdependently with the emotional relationships between an infant and its caregivers. When distress chronically rises above a level beyond which soothing can be provided interpersonally, the infant relies upon its own idiosyncratic solutions.

The British psychoanalyst Joan Symington writes:

The baby holds himself together in a variety of ways. He may focus his attention on a sensory stimulus—visual, auditory, tactile, or olfactory. When his attention is held by this stimulus he feels held together. He may engage in constant bodily movement which then feels like a continuous holding skin: if the movement stops, this may feel like a gap, a hole in the skin through which the self may spill out. An adult's pacing up and down to help contain anxiety is a remnant of this continuous movement. A third method consists of muscular tightening, a clenching together of particular muscle groups and maintaining them in this rigid position. This is an attempt physically to hold everything so tightly together that there can be no gap through which the spilling might occur. (1985, p. 481)

Symington's observations help to show a potential continuity from infancy to adulthood. The infantile origins of some of the unconscious ways of coping with unmentalized pain probably arise through the defensive deployment of attention.

From a Buddhist point of view, captured attention is an ordinary part of everyday experience. At any point during any day our attention is to some degree captured. The Buddhist view of captured attention suggests that we are never fully present to our experiences. Captured attention is ordinarily benign because when necessary we can shift and reclaim our attention in order to take in new information and adjust to new demands or opportunities of the moment.

The Vietnamese master Thich Nhat Hanh writes:

> We drink a cup of tea, but we do not know we are drinking a cup of tea. We sit with the person we love, but we do not know that she is sitting there. We walk, but we are not really walking. We are someplace else, thinking about the past or the future. The horse of our habit energy is carrying us along, and we are its captive. (1998, p. 25)

These words convey, in a condensed way, a basic but profound point. It is a constant challenge to recognize and repeatedly recover a state of presence and awareness, to shift from nowhere to now-here. I suggest that both psychoanalysis and meditation sponsor a continual movement back and forth between nowhere and now-here. We are constantly engaged in freeing attention from habits and intensities that trap or capture it.

Both psychotherapy and meditation can help to train the mind and to practice bringing attention to how we process pain. In psychotherapy, pain is investigated interpersonally. We strive to find an emotional language to describe and transform the experience of pain. We hope to free people from both subjective and actual isolation and to help them stop hiding from and hating their pain. As this attitude of investigating pain is internalized, it can be relied upon as an attitude, a skillful way of relating to experience, one that, with enough mindfulness and intention, can be called upon at any moment. A brief vignette illustrates this point.

Investigating Anger

A patient with a history of violent anger was also a serious Buddhist practitioner. I'll call him Brian. During one of his psychotherapy sessions Brian told me a story involving an incident from the previous weekend. He had gone to a party where he was aggressively insulted by another man and nearly provoked into a fistfight. Having been in many violent fights over the span of his life, Brian was not afraid of physical violence. However, he could, he reported, in that heated moment, question the wisdom of giving in to the impulse to fight. He spoke of deciding to leave the event and returning home where he sat down to meditate in order to try to calm himself. He told me how he could consciously feel the hatred pulsing through him and how he had imagined ridding himself of it by pounding it into the man who provoked him. His body was literally shaking with rage, he said, something I had also seen in some of our sessions together. The atmosphere of violence is electric, even when merely being recalled. Brian reported sitting in the rage until gradually his body began to soften. He began to breath more deeply, to unclench his jaws and fists, and his shoulders, legs, and back became relaxed.

Later during the same night Brian was startled awake by a disturbing telephone call from the same individual who had provoked him at the party. The caller again insulted Brian and dared him to meet him at an empty parking lot early in the morning to settle their score. His rage ignited again by the intrusive telephone call and the intense aggressive insults, my patient agreed to the meeting. He dressed and, powered by a sense of righteous indignation, went to his driveway to start his car. He fully intended to confront the individual and perhaps to kill him. Then he paused. It is this split second, the space between two thoughts, that sometimes makes the difference in the path of a lifetime. Sitting in the car, my patient said he thought about me and about the Buddhist teachings he was struggling so sincerely to live by. As he sat there he considered the years of suffering his own rage had rained down upon him and others. He thought, too, about how much rage and suffering his enemy must feel without any insight into it or any way of working directly with it. He went back inside his house and again began to meditate, this time chanting a compassion mantra until his hatred again began to fade. As he told this story to me, I felt the tangible presence of this man's already deep and expanding realization of loving kindness toward himself and toward his enemy. I felt close to tears with pride and inspiration at the way, through attention, he had turned his own rage into an active act of peacemaking. In an instant Brian had traveled from nowhere to now-here. This is a journey we must learn to make again and again.

From Nowhere to Now-Here

When pain cannot be successfully transformed from distress into comfort, it captures attention, creating what I call the need for *nowhere states of mind*. Nowhere states of mind tend to lead to isolation, sealing the individual off from relational contact, and protecting him, or so he imagines, from the turbulence of intense emotional experiences. Nowhere states may be vivid virtual worlds of pleasure or power or flat landscapes of psychic deadness. They offer illusory refuge from the experience of untransformed distress. Nowhere states of mind, in varying degrees of intensity, are ubiquitous. They seem to be part of the nature of having a mind that registers pain.

Irene

I was very close to my maternal grandmother, Irene. I spent much of my childhood in her presence. She was, for me, a refuge from the emotional pain and confusion of my family's complicated and difficult life. She died of cancer when I was eighteen. I helped to nurse her throughout the last year of her life. I watched her deteriorate little by little. Although busy with many activities as a senior in high school, I spent many hours at her bedside each week. I read to her as her eyes failed. I combed her thin white hair as she lost it. I changed her bedpan and held her hands when she wept from humiliation. I participated, with a kind of dazed attention, as she tried to cope with her intense frustration at and fear of being sick and dying.

As I had done with much of the pain in my family life, I pretended to be stronger and more confident than I really felt inside. This is what I saw my grandmother doing. And this is what I had learned to do unconsciously from my mother and father. Much of the time I nearly fooled myself into thinking that I could handle anything. I learned to deaden my most intense feelings, fearing, I suppose, that they might frighten or overwhelm my parents. I have lived much of my life against a kind of background of mild dissociation, struggling to be present, but being, in reality, deeply alienated from the details and textures of my actual emotional experience, lost in ever more distant nowhere states of mind. So it has been as an adult that I have learned to emerge from nowhere to now-here.

That whole year my grandmother was dying I wished intensely, in such a childlike way, to be able to figure out some way to help my grandmother recover. One night, sitting in the living room while my parents silently read the newspaper, I started to cry violently and uncontrollably. The sense of helplessness I had been unconsciously denying flooded over me. There was nothing I could think, do, wish, or command that would bring my grandmother's strength back or heal her cancer. I recognized this with a kind of shattering clarity. But I had no way to process the truth of this recognition, no way to think about it or put it into words. I remember a terrible feeling of shame and loneliness as my parents tried anxiously to comfort me, telling me that things would be all right. Gradually my familiar nowhere state of mind closed in around me, to protect me, again.

I became very depressed after my grandmother died. I tried to put it all behind me as a new freshman leaving home for the first time to go to college. The next few years were very hard for me personally, though at the time I could hardly admit that. What I am calling nowhere states of mind protected me from much of the turbulence I might have experienced had I been more open to emotional development and discovery and all the new tasks that I faced at that period in my life.

Reclaiming Attention

Psychoanalysis, like Buddhism, can well be described as a process that helps to reclaim attention from a multitude of idiosyncratically sponsored nowhere states of mind. The great intimacy of psychoanalysis can come from the shared project of working together to transform pain. In order to make this possible, the therapist must somehow woo patients into choosing attention, turning toward their fear, and moving directly into the experience of pain, rather than fighting it or sealing it off. There is no formula for this delicate task, although its effect can be felt in the growing conviction on the part of the analyst and the patient that such an investigation is worth attempting and can be survived over and over again by both parties as it is lived from moment to moment against the developing background of actual compassion and heart-fullness. Gradually, one learns that surprise can bring joy, which comes as a revelation.

It sounds counterintuitive to recommend learning to observe pain. Isn't that masochistic? Or sadistic, if you are watching another suffer? Won't focusing attention on the experience of pain make it worse? Actually, just the opposite is often true. Pain becomes unbearable to the degree that we actively fight against it. Denial of pain creates impasse. Hatred of the often shameful feelings that seem to arise around painful experience only compounds the sense of helplessness and fear. Psychotherapy and Buddhism provide the special conditions necessary to begin to observe pain with compassionate attention and to gradually transform the experience of it. This process, when successful, sponsors a growing confidence in the ability relate to pain. Joy in living moment to moment punctures the long-held dream of yearned-for safety and one feels subject to a kind of awful poignancy and immediacy. Sometimes experience is momentarily so crisp, so shockingly clear, so simultaneously fierce and delicate that tears are the only natural reply. Then one can find a sense of growing momentum that allows for a deeper embrace of the experience of being now-here.

The Preciousness of Life

My experience with my grandmother demonstrated, in powerful ways, that death was an indigestible fact in my own life as a young man. Instead of helping me appreciate the preciousness of life, my initial encounters with death drove me deeply into painful, alienated, nowhere states of mind.

Teachings on the inevitability of death are an important part of Buddhism. One way of looking at Buddhist practice is as a lifelong preparation for death. Though this may sound morbid, the intent is to help a person become more fully alive in the here and now. Buddhism emphasizes the transience of all experience. Nothing lasts. This fact is called the teaching of impermanence. It is often said that without a clear and frank awareness of death one does not feel with keenness, poignancy, and gratitude, the preciousness of life. This is not a sentimental point of view. The realization of the reality of death inspires a growing appreciation for this very moment.

Anita

Anita had also been a very important person to me while growing up. I remember with vivid fondness the atmosphere of her house, set on a large lot near the woods. There were many books, along with African rugs and artifacts, two elderly Siamese cats with striking eyes, homespun wool, and the ubiquitous smell of warm, freshly baked bread. Anita loved to garden as well as to cook. She would cut into a newly baked loaf of bread, and I would sit and visit and linger in the kitchen to talk while she cooked. She cared about history and politics. She loved nature and animals and ecology. She seemed very different from all the suburban mothers of my friends. When I was at Anita's house I glimpsed hints of life's wider possibilities and how interesting the world might actually be. Anita was one of the few adults I knew that made me look forward to growing up. While my grandmother had helped me to feel safe and protected, Anita enlivened my sense of possibility. I admired her.

After her children grew up and left home, Anita and her husband, a teacher, divorced and I did not see her for many years. One day she called me to tell me that she was dying. She wanted me to know, she said, how much our relationship had meant to her. She was calling all of her friends, she explained, in order to say goodbye. I responded with tears to her simple and direct message of love and caring. I think I was amazed that she had kept me in mind all those intervening years and that she would choose to include me in the intimate and painful experience of her cancer.

Buddhism had become important to Anita in the last years of her life, especially through the work of Stephen Levine. Also during these years Anita was working with Southeast Asian refugees. She helped them to find homes and jobs and education and, in turn, was influenced by their experiences. So many had lost nearly everything. They had no homes, no property; families had been separated or destroyed. They were living examples of what Buddha taught about the actuality of impermanence. Yet, for many, there was a strength and determination to begin again, despite their intense losses and suffering.

The experiences Anita had with her friends helped to inspire her and to prepare her for her death in an open, honest way. The brief time I was able to spend with her face to face at the end of her life made a deep impression on me. Unlike my grandmother, who felt helpless and humiliated by her illness, Anita had an unusual presence while facing her death. She described to me in exacting detail the progress of her illness, the course of her treatments, and the many emotions she had struggled with over the months since her diagnosis.

Her honesty and directness were at first disorienting. She gently explained that she had much to say and little time to say it in. She said she was much better at dealing with the psychological pain than with the physical pain. She said that it helped to talk about her experience with people and that she wanted me to know what she was going through. She had many friends helping her and her children supporting her. She said if I was uncomfortable with her directness she could understand that. She would stop talking about these things if I asked her to. I asked her not to. We talked about many happy memories and I told her about the changes and directions in my life. The last conversation we had was the day before she died. She was just back from the hospital again. I talked with her by phone and we said a final goodbye.

My experience with the way Anita faced her cancer has become a turning point in my life. It helped me to realize how an ordinary person can face their fear and reach out with love, even in the midst of death. I began to realize that it might be possible to investigate and to accept my own experiences much more deeply and consciously. Inertia is powerful. The habits of doubt and shame grow unless checked. Anita helped me to realize that the disturbing experiences of death and grief can be faced with courage, clarity, and openness. Over the years, I have chosen to read the work of many Buddhist teachers. I doubt I would have made these choices or have been drawn to the richness of Buddhist thought without having been pointed in this direction by Anita. The seeds she helped to plant have taken root and grown. Anita instructed me to look into Buddhism. She said, "There's something there that I think you'll really get if you look." I often remind myself, thinking of Anita, "Go ahead Jeff, face your fear." Courage, I'm learning, is ordinary and a matter of how we learn to use our attention.

End Piece

It is traditional to dedicate whatever merit an activity has to all sentient beings, with the hope that the activity will, even if in a small way, contribute to the lessening of the suffering of all beings in the universe. I dedicate this essay to Anita, to my grandmother, to my wife Kay, to my parents, and to my friends, teachers, and patients, as well as to all sentient beings.

As Pema Chodron writes:

It is never too late for us to look at our minds. We can always sit down and allow the space for anything to arise. Sometimes we have a shocking experience of ourselves. Sometimes we try to hide. Sometimes we have a surprising experience of ourselves. Often we get carried away. Without judging, without buying into the likes and dislikes, we can always encourage ourselves to just be here again and again and again. (1997, p. 27)

CHAPTER SIX

A Fruitful Harvest:
Some Notes on Dreaming

[W]hat of the fruitful harvest of those dreams which succeed in grasping the nettle of mental pain, resolving a conflict, relinquishing an untenable position? We will surely wish our hypothesis about dream-life to shed some light on this question of growth.

— Donald Meltzer, *The Claustrum*

FOR DONALD MELTZER, DREAMING IS AT THE CENTER of the psychoanalytic experience. He links the exploration of dreams with the efficacy of the psychoanalytic process. Exploring dream-life helps us to get a glimpse of the way dreaming contributes to what Meltzer calls "the question of growth." Here, I offer some personal reflections, inspired by Meltzer, while also departing from him, at times, on the fruitful harvest of dreams and dreaming.

The Second Life of Dreaming

What is the fate of the dream, the thing-in-itself, upon waking? The situation is simple: the dream has vanished. In fact, we never remember our dreams. Upon waking, we can collect only bits of evidence that the dream was recently alive and wandering among us. The fragments and details, the emotions, and the unpredictable residues that linger from the inventiveness of our dream-life are like the skeletal traces of a fabulous lost beast. The dream itself can never be recovered, relived, or represented in any complete way.

Dreaming creates what can be poetically called "a country of the mind," a place where we can go, usually while asleep, to yield full attention to psychic reality. In this new country we can live a second life while dreaming. This second life may become a laboratory where unconscious experiments in living and feeling are carried out each night. While we dream problems are pictured, solutions are sought, alternatives are realized, and emotions and memories are tasted and tested in ways that may not be available during waking life.

Watching children play is perhaps as close as we can come to observing a dream being made. Dreaming may be seen as a form of unconscious play. The child playing *makes a scene* populated with characters, actions, backgrounds, intentions, conflicts, and rapid transformations of ideas, fantasies, and emotions.

Something similar goes on in dreaming. The concreteness of the experience of entering a dream scene lends the experience emotional power, while the transience of dreaming makes the realization of myriad circumstances possible.

Even violent impulses can be safely expressed in play and dreaming because there is a mysterious process of symbolization developing—an atmosphere that children call "just pretend" and that adults call "just a dream."

Dreaming, then, like playing, opens up a space of psychic freedom. Somehow, something troubling, or something new, or even something reaching toward us from the future makes its way into the dream scene and, from there, sometimes proceeds on into waking consciousness.

Through dreaming and the production of dream thoughts and events there is contact with a continuous unfolding unconscious conversation between the self and its own experiences. As one continues to dream night after night and year after year, autonomous symbols naturally emerge and the result is what the poet Shelley calls "an enlargement of the imagination."

Meltzer strongly emphasizes that we import meaning from one world (the dream laboratory) into another (the world of our waking lives). Dreaming leaves the gate to the psyche open every night and the emotions generated by dreaming wander back through and linger into the day.

The many experiences accumulated in the second life of dreaming influence our choices in waking life. Successful dreaming means that less pain must be hidden in the body, projected into the group, or split off, denied, and located in other objects or dimensions. Through the intimate exploration of the patient's dreams, shared in the analytic encounter, waking and dreaming processes begin to cooperate. Contact with dream-life, paradoxically, helps one to grow a wider tolerance and deeper respect for the facts of external reality.

Grasping the Nettle

According to Meltzer, there is always one important question present at the beginning of every treatment: *Who shall have the pain?* In the analytic setting we can observe that some people turn toward the analyst, hoping to find someone capable of tolerating the expression of painful emotions. Other people turn away, overtly rejecting the possibility of glimpsing, feeling, facing, and sharing their emotional pain.

There are, of course, many obstacles to sharing emotional pain. Some patients report that they cannot dream, or that they cannot recall their dreams. Some claim that their dreams mean nothing. Still others hate their dreams—or are terrified to go to sleep, hoping at all costs to avoid having a dream. Some patients seem convinced that, at a deep level, revealing the truth of their suffering can only lead to punishment. And, finally, in some situations, people expect awareness of the pain so vividly made present by certain kinds of dreams to excite and stimulate cruelty in the minds and actions of others.

Selves absorb the impacts *of* dreams, for better or worse. Dreams devolve into nightmares and into night terrors. These shocks and insults accumulate over dozens of nights with no sense of relief or rescue. What happens if, for some, dreaming is more difficult to bear than waking life? People can be haunted by their dreams. Dreams can be traumatic objects; you can feel injured not just *in* your dreams but *by* your dreams. No wonder some people hate the experience of dreaming and even of having a mind that dreams.

Yet painful dreams can also be important beginnings. When a person is unable to ask or formulate the question of *Who shall have the pain?* his or her dream may be capable of giving form to the question instead. Dreams bring psychic reality directly into the foreground and allow the question of *Who shall have the pain?* to emerge and to seek an adequate reply.

Now I want to share an example of such a dream. I'm neither presenting a case study nor offering an analysis of the patient's dream. I present the dream simply as a specimen of the emergence of *the intensity of mental pain* in the early months of an analysis.

> I am in a crowded street somewhere and there is an evil force coming toward me. I can't see it or hear it but I know it is there, and getting closer. Horrible things are happening all around me. Women and kids are dying in horrible ways. I have a mirror or something and somehow I'm supposed to use it to fend off this "thing." It is getting closer and closer and I know something terrible is going to happen.

The figures and events, the objects and emotions that emerge in dreams like this one are painful to register and intimidating to behold. The intensity of the dream strains both the analyst and the patient. Yet at the same time such dreams are really gifts if one can find the psychic space necessary to welcome their intensity.

If it can become possible to turn toward the dream, it can become a *shared object* that takes on its own life between the patient and the analyst. The shared dream (and the pain) can then be explored against a new background of gradually expanding spacious awareness generated by a dreaming couple.

To me, this is the heart of the therapeutic action of psychoanalysis: the discovery of a symbolizing couple and the expansion of it in the interaction between analyst and analysand through a process that can become repeatedly internalized and elaborated within the patient's own dream life.

The Background of Dreams

I value dream life. I encourage my patients to pay attention to their dreams, to report on them, and to explore them with me in our sessions.

Over many years, I have heard many hundreds of dreams narrated by my patients and often, in an analysis lasting several years, I have the privilege to hear dozens if not hundreds of dreams from a single dreamer. From this richness of raw material, I have abstracted three domains that I think can meaningfully organize one dimension of the analyst's listening strategy when approaching the significance of any patient's dream life.

I've come to believe that we must pay more attention to the background of people's lives and experiences. The context and setting of every experience is important, including, perhaps especially, the background of dreams. The background of the dream offers a different kind of information than the objects of the dream or the actions of the characters in the foreground do. Deliberately slowing down and focusing on the background of the dream helps to bring other dimensions of psychic reality into the foreground of attention for both the patient and the analyst.

The background may be an indicator of profound psychic stress, conflict, or the emergence of new psychic functions. It has, I suggest, three general *domains*. I see these domains as patterns within the larger, more elusive and mysterious process of unconscious symbol-formation that becomes observable through the development of a deepening analytic process.

I want to contextualize this conjecture in relation to Meltzer's description of life in the Claustrum. It is possible that the background of dreams may show evidence of life in the Claustrum and the corresponding attitudes associated with the compartments of the internal mother. The domains that I am proposing, however, refer more generally to all dreams, not just to dreams in which the subject is living inside an internal object through intrusive identification.

I will offer three more dreams from the same patient described earlier to briefly illustrate my speculation. I recognize here that I am both departing from Meltzer's views and too briefly offering my own, and that in order to be thoroughly convincing these ideas will require greater elaboration in a future discussion. Nonetheless, I want to open these new avenues for thought even if they are thus far only partially travelled.

Survival

I was driving a truck, a real beater, and even though I was not going over the speed limit, everything felt really shaky. Then, all of the sudden, the road collapsed and I and all the others cars plunged into a gigantic hole. I just kept falling, there was no bottom. I woke up and I couldn't go back to sleep.

Survival is an existential life problem of the organism or individual. The dreams in this domain picture profound psychic distress. They have to do, I think, with the unconscious memory of the problem of the viability of the organism in relationship to the environment.

These are areas described by Winnicott as "primitive agonies" and by Bion as "nameless dreads." I believe that such dreams suggest evidence of a situation Bion named "infantile catastrophe." I am also impressed by Tustin's descriptions of the earliest impacts of the premature awareness of separation. I describe all these kinds of agonies as linked by an experience of *primal exposure*. This is a state of unthinkable vulnerability characterized by the awareness, however rudimentary or intuitive, of the absence of protection from annihilation. In other words, the preconception of not existing has been stimulated much too early for the individual to be able to use it as an inauguration into thinking through and elaborating this particular reality.

One solution to the presence of such primal exposure may be intrusion, through projective identification, into an internal object, as Meltzer has so compellingly described. But that is only one possible fate. I believe dreams in this domain convey the beginning stages of a process that is attempting to make the unthinkable thinkable through picturing experiences (in Bion's Grid, via row C images) of catastrophic background events.

As an individual's dream life evolves, we may discern plausible patterns that suggest how the person has unconsciously coped with their own personal primal catastrophe. Dreams such as the one just mentioned reveal that the patient feels he is missing what I call a reliable *floor for experience*. Without such a floor the very possibility of survival is called into question.

I believe that being able to pick up on this dimension of the background of a dream is crucial in establishing for the patient not only a feeling of being understood, but also the potential for a feeling of faith that it is possible and worthwhile for the analytic couple to face such intimidating pains and to go forward together. It is through risking sharing these disturbing images and the sensations and affects that they carry and open up that a gradual trust in the reality of an emotional floor for experience can be discovered and built.

Adaptation

> I'm standing on a stage with a group of men with a giant Nazi flag behind us. I'm wearing a Nazi uniform. I'm giving the Heil Hitler salute with everyone else. I'm terrified people will see that my heart's not really in it.

The theme of adaptation has, of course, a long and complex history. The concept is central in biological and evolutionary sciences as well as in some streams of psychoanalysis, especially in ego psychology. As I am using the term, the dreams in this domain have to do with the struggle to create personal meaning versus complying with (or being dominated by) the family and the group. Obviously an immense and complex array of issues is involved in such a theme. Obstacles to intimacy and sincere expression are often pictured. Patients describe feelings of helplessness and frustration that coexist with thwarted initiative. The patient worries about things like selling out, settling for less, cutting his losses, being a coward, playing the fool, and running out of time.

Once the patient's issue of survival has been adequately addressed in the analytic process by successfully creating an emotional floor for experience, the next domain often involves entering the profound realm of adaptation to the family, the group, the community, and even to a particular moment in history. The environment can then be explored as a multitude of variables that both constrain and facilitate the development of the self. Within it, emotions are patterned and processed through the challenges of adaptation and through increasingly personal interaction with the environment, which sponsors learning and maturation across the life span. Dreams help show the history of this process as well as its progress.

Thriving

> I'm in a beautiful place in the mountains with a woman I am in love with. I have some kind of arithmetic problem I'm trying to solve. I'm trying to write it out on a large piece of paper on the ground. The woman offers to help me and I let her. I wake up with a feeling of incredible happiness.

The dreams in this domain have to do with learning to trust one's own internal objects, letting them be free, and establishing a space for creativity where one can harvest the fruits of intuition and welcome thoughts in search of a thinker.

To outline a model of the factors that promote thriving is beyond the scope of this chapter. However, I think we can say that the development of an apparatus for thinking, feeling, and experiencing is seen as crucial, and that it is regarded as a process that can grow beyond the stage of merely solving the problems of survival and social and emotional adaptation. Bion emphasized what he called the K-link, which he saw as a robust curiosity to get-to-know about and investigate the vast scope of the mystery of creation, life, and the universe. Grotstein has taken this yearning to learn about life in an ever fuller way seriously and has helped us appreciate the motive force of a "truth instinct" that I think is linked to the subjective orientation I'm calling "thriving." —taton

Dreams give us glimpses and preconceptions of thriving, as well as, over the course of our work—and with careful attention—clues to the structure of the personality that can enable it to creatively thrive and learn from experience. Here I believe that to some degree thriving implies going beyond self and emotion and beginning to consider one's relationship to what Bion called O, an unknowable, absolute reality that is the ultimate background for all our dreams and experiences.

The Analyst's Own Dreams as a Guide

I want to briefly describe how a dream helped me to symbolize the emotional impact on me of my relationship to a young schizophrenic patient whom I'll call Andy. I will also describe how this dream guided me in making deeper communicative contact with him.

When I first met Andy, he was thin, disheveled, and haunted looking. Andy told me he spent most of his days in bed "under cover." He said he enjoyed daydreaming. This intense activity seemed to insulate him from very powerful feelings of persecution. I vividly remember a session, for example, where Andy felt so persecuted that he threatened to break the window in order to escape.

His communications sometimes flowered into religious delusions of intense grandiosity. He believed, for example, that he had been secretly placed at the center of a giant cosmic net and had been chosen to absorb the pain of the entire world. His job was to filter the pain of millions of lives through his own body and mind.

In the early months of our work Andy often withdrew into wordlessness. He would sit in the corner of the couch, slumped and silent. He would not look at me. In the silence I often noted feelings of helplessness, frustration, and sometimes extreme anxiety in my body. I also had the feeling that I might suddenly fall asleep.

I understood all these experiences as elements of intense projective identifications. The question I struggled with was how to find words for any of this experience and how to share my understanding with Andy.

One night I dreamt:

I am standing outside a tall round brick tower that looks as if it is part of a castle. I go inside and climb a steep circular stone staircase. At the top of the stairs is a small round room with windows. In the middle of the room is a table and on the table is a hunk of clay on a pedestal. Next to it is a computer screen. As I watch the clay begins to form itself into a human head, with the face of a man. I feel sudden incredible fear flood me. The clay is making itself into something. Then I notice that the process is being represented on the computer screen, which also shows the picture of the clay face. This makes me curious and I'm aware of both fear and curiosity powerfully combined. When the clay is fully formed I become even more frightened. Now I feel an enormous force coming from inside the empty eyes of the clay face. I feel I am being physically sucked into the clay head and that I will be trapped inside. I wake in terror.

I was relieved to wake up. But I had a strongly uncanny feeling. I had a bizarre and disorienting feeling *in my body*. The atmosphere of the dream lingered for a long time. I thought, "*This is Andy's dream!*"

Upon reflection, it seemed that this dream might be about my experience of the conscious and unconscious impact I was ambivalently trying to welcome as I got to know Andy. The dream, I felt, was showing me what it was like unconsciously for me to be with Andy.

Another way of looking at the dream is to say that my contact with Andy introduced me to a split-off psychotic element of my own personality. Spending time with Andy invited this new "character" to enter my dream theater and to inaugurate an improbably intimate conversation with psychosis. Unconsciously, I was trying very hard to make sense of what schizophrenic experience is really like.

There came a moment in a subsequent session with Andy where he again withdrew into silence. I waited for several minutes and during that time the atmosphere of my dream returned spontaneously. I had not planned to make an interpretation based upon my dream, but drawing on that experience, I said something like, "I wonder if you're afraid to look at me because you fear that if you do something terrible will happen. Looking at my face might feel overwhelming. You're afraid something powerful will take you over and trap you. Maybe there just are no words for such awful things."

Andy now looked directly at me. Suddenly, he found his voice. He told me, in a very lucid way, about a night at the state hospital. He said he had been given a shot and had terrible cramps that paralyzed him. He remembered feeling that he just wanted to die. He described being taken to a locked ward where he later witnessed a patient assaulted by another patient. He said he did not speak for days after that.

A mother cannot dream her infant's dream. But she can dream her own dream about what it must be like to be her infant. This does not give her access to her infant's subjectivity in the sense that she can know it directly, completely, or transparently. But her infant's experience can be meaningful to her in a deeply imagined and embodied way. When she shares that meaning, made from the inside out, the song and dance of her voice and actions carry intuitions that awaken her infant's preconceptions about what contact with the mind of another might ultimately make possible. In its own way, this is the genuine fruitful harvest that the psychoanalytic setting seeks to make possible—an intimate contact with psychic reality that can be shared with another, like the experience of a dream.

CHAPTER SEVEN

The Poisoned Link:
A Second Look at Envy

NVY IS AN UNPLEASANT TOPIC. AS A CONCEPT, IT immediately raises controversial issues. As a living reality, it is hard to think about, hard to talk about, and hard to work with.

Since as a clinician I have not been able to help everyone who comes to see me, I have asked myself, "How might envy play a role in this situation?" Why do some treatments break down or end in impasse? Is the obstacle in the patient? Is it in me? Is it in the link between us? These practical questions deserve attention.

To explore such questions I decided to review some of my cases using the lens of envy to reflect on how things get stuck. After pursuing this for some time, I felt a new interest in wrestling with the reality of envy as a human experience.

When I began my process of reflection, envy was a blind spot. Now my intention is to share the evolution of my second look at envy. I briefly describe and differentiate the concept as it has evolved in the Kleinian and post-Kleinian tradition. Then, while I do not present a case study, I instead offer two brief clinical vignettes to link theory with actual experience.

The Concept of Envy

Clinical experience has compelled me to recognize that the envy and destructiveness that Klein, Bion, Rosenfeld, Segal, and Joseph (among others) have all contributed toward identifying is not merely a conceptual matter. Their descriptions are attempts to comprehend powerful, energetic, intimidating emotional forces. Such forces can prevent people from being able to use the help that is offered. Sometimes such forces actively destroy a potentially constructive therapeutic situation.

The concept of envy centers on damage done to the experience of goodness. According to the Kleinian analyst Robert Caper (1988), "In psychoanalytic terms, envy is felt to damage or destroy the good object, and, at the same time, the parts of the ego that are linked to the good object" (p. 220).

Melanie Klein felt that destructive envy had infantile origins. Marco Chiesa (2001), in an excellent essay in a collection titled *Kleinian Theory: A Contemporary Perspective*, explains in detail Klein's view of envy and its destructive consequences:

> Although early experience of deprivation and other traumatic environmental experiences are important factors in enhancing and stimulating envy, Klein makes it clear that the envious attacks are fundamentally directed towards the good and gratifying primary object.... The good object is resented and hated because it is endowed with life-giving qualities which the baby depends on for his survival. The baby gradually realizes that the source of good experiences of feeding and comforting is an external object. Under the influence of envy the baby wishes first to possess the good qualities of the object and then, when he realizes that this is unobtainable, to attack and spoil the good experience and the object itself.... The spoiling of the good experience results in great difficulties in taking and keeping inside one's mind (introjecting) good and benign objects. (p. 95)

In my clinical experience, I have met one man who seemed to embody this description completely. I will call him Mr. A. He was an intelligent, middle-aged man who radiated suffering. However, he completely disowned his experience of extreme emotional pain. Being with him (several sessions a week) was further complicated by his violent contempt and withering attacks upon any attempt to understand his experience.

For example, in a typical session, after I had made an interpretation that seemed to momentarily establish an empathic connection, he described attending a business meeting with his colleagues and his boss. He said:

> The meeting was at a country club. I guess you'd call it nice. The food was nothing to write home about. The wine was cheap. I would be embarrassed to serve wine like that. It probably came from a cardboard box. The poor bastards who belong to these places really think it means something. Don't waste your time dreaming. You sit on a waiting list for years to have the privilege of being rejected. No one gets in because they actually deserve it. This best and brightest stuff is bullshit. Once you get in there's nothing worth waiting for. Everyone still has to crap and wipe their ass afterward. But those poor bastards think their shit smells like perfume.

Although this session occurred many years ago I can still feel some of the tension in my body as I recall our many difficult meetings. I can now see that one important way of understanding this kind of communication is that Mr. A. was always unconsciously describing his experience of being with me.

Let me offer one potential way of making meaning of this fragment from a Kleinian point of view. There is a very brief unconscious acknowledgement that there is a "nice" feeling between us. But almost instantly this nice feeling is transformed into a complaint about the cheap "interpretations" given to Mr. A. The implication is that I probably say the same sort of thing to all my patients regardless of their emotional experience.

The atmosphere of the session rapidly decays and Mr. A. feels as if he is being evaluated so that he can be excluded. If Mr. A. admits his desire for emotional contact he fears he will find there is nothing here of value. Also, there are feelings of elitism, idealization, denigration, and grandiosity that are projected and interfere with the possibility of making a connection with a person potentially sensitive to Mr. A.'s deep and wordless feelings of pain.

Mr. A. was often unable to differentiate between his psychic reality and the ways that it colored and spoiled his experience of the outside world. His envious attacks stripped experience of all goodness, leaving him either in a barren emotional wasteland, or, worse yet, in a hostile psychic environment surrounded by damaged, destroyed, and violently retaliating objects.

In his review of Klein's *Envy and Gratitude,* Winnicott (1959) tells a different story about the origins of infantile distress. He affirms the value of Klein's description of envy as a factor that appears in the psychoanalysis of patients like Mr. A., but he takes issue with the use of the term envy to describe the infant's earliest relationship to an object. He writes, "For me the word 'envy' implies a high degree of sophistication, that is to say a degree of ego-organization in the subject which is not present at the beginning of life" (p. 444).

Winnicott goes on to explain:

> At the beginning, as I see it, the infant's relationship to an object is so intimately bound up with the presentation of the object to the infant that the two cannot be separated. In terms of object-relationships the infant is entirely dependent on the way each bit of the world is brought to the infant, so that one can say that the world is presented to the infant *either* in such a way that the object seems to be created by the instinctual drive in the infant *or* else in such a way that there is no link between the creative element in the infant and the existence of the external object. (p. 445)

In Klein's version of the earliest relationship to the object, it is the dawning recognition of separateness that paves the way for the infant to sense its dependence upon the generosity of the object in sharing its goodness. Klein asserts that this realization stimulates envy and subsequently an attack on the source of the goodness.

Winnicott, on the other hand, emphasizes the conditions that sponsor the creation of a link between what we can speak of as the creative element in the infant and the recognition of the "existence" of the external object. Instead of emphasizing a destructive attack on the object, Winnicott suggests that the inability to make and elaborate a creative link arises if there is too much premature awareness of separation that is felt as impingement that must be defended against.

These two points of view are not necessarily mutually exclusive. While Mr. A. seemed to embody a continuous attack upon goodness, he also, in hindsight, felt exiled from being able to have any creative link exist, either within or outside, and be recognized. He was, I think, desperate to find out if he could share his emotions with another person. However, the very desire to share his experience immediately stimulated envious attacks as well as terrors of separateness and of the damage he might do to the other.

A vicious mixture of envy and ego-destructive shame seemed to overwhelm Mr. A., making it impossible for him find any kind of resting place, either on his own or with another person. This circumstance left Mr. A. feeling profoundly excluded from ordinary human relations, thus further fueling his envy.

A Post-Kleinian Point of View

Now I want to introduce a post-Kleinian point of view. First I will describe Bion's perspective, then an important reformulation of envy proposed by Meltzer. You will notice a shift in perspective in the movement from viewing envy as a struggle between love and destructiveness to a post-Kleinian expansion of this conflict, seen now as a struggle between emotion and anti-emotion. Another way one might describe this shift is as a struggle between emotional aliveness and psychic deadness.

Commentators like Lopez-Corvo (2003, 2006) and Sandler (2005) agree that Bion used the term envy in the same spirit that Klein did. But Bion adds significantly to Klein's model. In expanding the dynamism between paranoid-schizoid and depressive anxieties and defenses, Bion builds a theory of thinking, learning, and communication not found in Klein's model.

Bion's (1962) ideas about alpha function, maternal reverie, and the transformation of sensation into psychical qualities, as well as on the further permutations of a container–contained structure, bring multiple variables together to create a model of psychic function that can interdependently generate experience from moment to moment.

Additionally, Bion describes the establishment of what he termed links in the realm of emotions, in particular love, hate, and curiosity.

Envy is an emotion that interferes with the nascent self's ability to establish links of this sort with objects and the world. The placement of emotion and its fate at the center of the development of subjectivity opens the field to allow the recognition and appreciation of the complexity of each particular individual mind and its natural history.

It is important to appreciate Bion's shift of attention from the quality of the object to the quality of the link to the object. From one angle, the absence of the link is even more important than its presence. Bion (1970) writes:

> The patient feels an absence of fulfillment of his desires. The absent fulfillment is experienced as a 'no-thing'. The emotion aroused by the 'no-thing' is felt as indistinguishable from the 'no-thing'. The emotion is replaced by a 'no emotion'.... 'Non-existence' immediately becomes an object that is immensely hostile and filled with murderous envy towards the quality or function of existence wherever it is found. (pp. 19–20)

It takes some careful attention and imagination to appreciate what Bion is trying to describe in this very dense passage. Notice how the absence of fulfillment (intense frustration) generates a "no-thing" that in turn generates an emotion that is felt to be indistinguishable from the nothing experience. This emotion is further transformed into what Bion calls a "no-emotion." Then Bion describes the experience of this as "immensely hostile and filled with murderous envy towards the quality or function of existence." To me, this is a remarkably imaginative description of a particular form of violent subjective experience.

Implicitly linked to this point of view is this thought of Meltzer's, in his 1988 essay "Concerning the Stupidity of Evil," where he writes:

> Clinical experience, particularly with young psychotic children, has suggested the theory of aesthetic conflict as a primal developmental event. The painful state of uncertainty about the congruence of the external form of objects (the beauty of the world) and the enigmatic interior qualities is defended against by splitting the passionate response. This is effected in the spirit of revulsion

from emotion itself.... Under this theory of emotion, which sees emotion confronted by anti-emotion rather than love confronted by hatred, Melanie Klein's formulation on envy finds a new base. I would formulate primal envy not as the breast-that-feeds-itself, for instance, but as an urge to interfere with the object's capacity for passionate experience, and thus with the relationship to truth. (pp. 562–63)

With this formulation, Meltzer reveals a deeper dynamic motivation for the perpetuation of envy. Contact with the other is the only way to grow and to learn from experience. However, genuine contact with another generates all kinds of emotion. As long as the subject maintains his revulsion toward emotion, whether in himself or in others, he will continue to envy the apparent ease and naturalness with which others can couple, communicate, creatively interact, or simply coexist.

To summarize, then, Klein introduced the importance of envy as an attack on goodness. Bion shows how envy can arise as a kind of destructiveness linked to violent intolerance of frustration, and Meltzer, finally, suggests that envy is a motivated interference with the "the object's capacity for passionate experience."

The Complexity of Envy in the Clinical Encounter

I would now like to try to link the depth of what Kleinians and post-Kleinians have understood about envy to the clinical encounter. I want to return to the questions that motivated this "second look" at envy. As I noted earlier, I wanted to better understand where the obstacles to helping a patient might arise. I thought the possibilities might be (1) in the patient, (2) in myself, and (3) in the link between us.

From a Kleinian point of view, I can try to speak to the patient's unconscious destructive activities, to the difficulty of containing these activities in my countertransference, and to the way these activities are lived out in the transference-countertransference matrix.

From the post-Kleinian point of view, I can further recognize that the unconscious motivation for envy may come from a deeper place of revulsion to emotion. This implies damage to or lack of development in the container–contained structure that Bion posits as necessary for the development of the capacity to think, feel, reflect, and experience.

The implication of such a damaged container–contained relationship is that the patient cannot take in and make use of the analyst's alpha function. To address this pragmatic dilemma, we must go one step further and consider the recent ideas of the Italian analyst Antonino Ferro. Ferro has developed the concept of "the bi-personal field," which focuses on the "unconscious phantasy of the couple." Ferro (1999) writes:

> The structure of this field is determined by the two mental lives and by criss-cross projective identifications passing back and forth between analyst and patient. It is expected, of course, that there will be a greater flow of projective identifications passing from the patient to the analyst. Periodically... the accumulation of criss-crossing projective identifications creates pockets of 're-sistance' in the couple (not in the patient!). These zones require special attention on the part of the analyst, who with his *second glance* must recognize and interpret such blind spots, as they are an obstacle to analytic progress. (p. 16)

To me, the significance of Ferro's work (along with that of such writers as Ogden, Grotstein, Bollas, and Modell) is that he provides ways to picture with greater precision the complex development of the container–contained process at multiple levels of interaction—including the intrapsychic, interpersonal, and intersubjective levels.

Most are familiar with the idea that the clinician must become a container for the patient's projective identifications. This is a complex process that much has been written about. When the clinician can function adequately in this task we can say he or she operates as a projective identification welcoming object. This function allows the patient to feel recognized emotionally. It sponsors what I regard as a primary emotional transformation from distress to comfort. Without the ability to move emotionally from distress to comfort it is impossible to focus attention and to seek out help from others.

When the clinician can reply to the patient's distress in a sincere and embodied way, there is a feeling of an emotional floor for experience being created together. As the container–contained interaction builds up interpersonally it is gradually introjectively identified with. This experience gradually sponsors the recognition of a background of safety, and with it an expansion of awareness and reflectiveness. But in addition—and here is the importance of Ferro's new focus on the bi-personal field—this growth of awareness and reflectiveness happens not only in the patient but also in the clinician, and, especially importantly, in the therapeutic couple. It is the couple that is developing the capacity to process more experience together.

Envy disrupts this process. It poisons the link to the object and drastically changes the emotional color of the developing psychoanalytic encounter. To return to Meltzer's thought, he offers, in addition to a description of envy's destructive consequences, another motivation for its perpetuation. If there is revulsion toward emotion, as he suggests, envy interferes with any link that generates emotion. Envy, then, becomes a way of blocking emotion by poisoning the link to the object before that emotion, regardless of the form it takes, can flourish.

This situation creates a crisis for the psychoanalytic couple. It is precisely the task of the couple to welcome difficult emotions, tolerate them, get to know them, and to experience them together. Following Ferro, I believe that the clinician must not become trapped in a rigidly dyadic view that collapses the field of potential experience. The essential problem is to find ways to welcome disturbing emotions and experiences into awareness, where they have some chance of being lived and processed by the couple.

In the transference, the clinician is at risk of concretely becoming a projective identification rejecting object. By that I mean that he or she cannot welcome with reverie the experience of envy or other difficult emotions. I shall give a very brief description of my work with Ms. B. to highlight this point.

Ms. B.

My work with Ms. B., who entered therapy in midlife, took place over several years. Her primary complaint was a feeling of being stuck in her life. She said she was "wasting away inside." She had recently ended a lengthy relationship with a woman because she could not decide to commit to her. She reported that she felt boxed in by her life.

In our sessions, Ms. B. spoke mostly about her complaints. She said she had no memories from childhood and was not able to remember her dreams. Sometimes she reported being moved by the pain and vulnerability she witnessed in others. For example, she might report a scene from a film she had watched—yet she quickly distanced herself from her emotions as they arose. If I showed curiosity about her experience she would clam up, or disown the experience, or even mock my interest.

Inevitably, after any emotional connection, Ms. B. would describe a process we called "murdering the moment." She claimed to hate this corrosive attitude but it persisted nonetheless. When the pain of self-awareness became too great, Ms. B. would retreat back into resigned isolation. She'd say with great irritation, "I've always been on my own and I like it better that way."

In one poignant session, Ms. B. described going to a cafe. As she was ordering a coffee, she observed a young lesbian couple sitting nearby. She described how they kissed and were talking with animation. Ms. B. said she was startled by the "radiance" of the women's faces. "They were beautiful," she said. Then she said, "They don't live like I do. They know some kind of secret. I want to know what they know."

At the time, I tried to understand Ms. B.'s experience in terms of envy. I interpreted her feeling of being left out and her idealization that there is a secret knowledge that she is deprived of. In hindsight, I feel I failed to open up a space for Ms. B. and for myself to feel the many potential different emotions latent in this experience. I boxed Ms. B. in, using my preformed meanings and concepts about what might be important rather than being open to explore what new feeling might be trying to emerge in her story and between us.

I now think the secret knowledge Ms. B. sensed and was trying to realize was the freedom to experience her emotion passionately. I missed the yearning, the impact of beauty, the hope for the future, the coming alive, and the hunger for recognition, including their reflection in the transference, of Ms. B.'s own complex emotionality trying to emerge. It was too easy for me to also get caught in a negative equilibrium and fear of change. Today I hope I would listen differently and more deeply to her story. I hope I could open up more of a play space or potential space to glimpse the many emotions trying to be admitted between us.

Ms. B. said, "I've always been on my own, and I like it better that way." Statements of this kind are a trap that the clinician, too, needs to be careful to avoid. Bion and Meltzer help us to glimpse that for certain people the struggle is not only between love and destructiveness. There is another level where emotion feels, unconsciously, to the couple like an invitation to a catastrophe. Revulsion toward emotion is driven not only by destructiveness. The illusory safety of an anti-emotion attitude toward life can infect the couple, poisoning the links to emotions as they arise and before they can be explored. My hope is that through recognizing this process it may be possible to transform the unconscious phantasy of the couple, making real psychic transformation possible again.

CHAPTER EIGHT

Paying Attention to Attention

W E PAY ATTENTION TO MANY DIFFERENT THINGS
throughout an ordinary day. We are so familiar with the
function of attention that we may fail to notice how much
a part of ordinary experience attention really is. Psychoanalysis directs
attention inward. In psychoanalysis the events of daily life are noticed
within a new context. We learn to pay attention to feelings, images,
dreams, fantasies, and to the recognition of emerging patterns and unconscious defenses. Attention helps link dream life and waking life. The
psychoanalyst Donald Meltzer (1983) states: "Attention is the tiller by
which we steer the organ of consciousness about in the teeming world of
psychic qualities" (p. 29).

Describing Attention

The human ability to investigate the life of attention yields surprising
complexity. Phenomenologically, many different *qualities* of attention
may be identified. Attention can be focused or dispersed. It can be split
and divided. It can be alternating or fixed. It can be full or depleted. One
can speak of attention being directed to both material and immaterial
objects. There are limits to how much one can keep in attention and for
how long one can maintain concentrated focus. William James (1890)
famously writes:

> Everyone knows what attention is. It is the taking possession by
> the mind ... of one ... of several simultaneously possible objects or

trains of thought.…It implies withdrawal from some things in order to deal effectively with others. (p. 75)

In beginning to describe attention, I am mindful of the fact that attention can be approached from many different points of view. Models of the nature and function of attention can be found in cognitive science and psychology, phenomenology, and the ancient multicultural traditions of meditation, as well as by way of psychoanalytic perspectives. Ultimately one might hope to understand the nature and function of attention more completely by competently drawing on each of these traditions. Here I shall be narrowly concerned with the role of attention in influencing the subjective quality of personal experience, drawing primarily on psychoanalytic sources.

In "Formulations Regarding the Two Principles in Mental Functioning," Freud (1911) defined attention in relationship to consciousness and to the "increased significance of external reality" that leads to a function of "passing judgement" about "whether a particular idea was true or false, that is … in agreement with reality" (p. 16). Freud writes:

A special function was instituted which had periodically to search the outer world in order that its data might be already familiar if an urgent inner need should arise; this function was *attention*. Its activity meets the sense-impressions half-way, instead of awaiting their appearance. At the same time there was probably introduced a system of *notation*, – whose task was to deposit the results of this periodical activity of consciousness—a part of that which we call *memory*. (p. 15)

Now, consider the formulation presented by the contemporary psychologists Greenberg and Snell (1997), who write:

[A] well-functioning attentional system must fulfill several tasks, including identification of important elements in the environment, the ability to ignore irrelevant stimuli while sustaining attention to the primary focus, the ability to access inactive memories, and the capacity to shift attention rapidly as the result of new information. (p. 108)

When read together these two descriptions appear very similar, despite the fact that they were written a hundred years apart. Yet the picture can be enlarged further. It is interesting to at least briefly consider attention from a neuroscience point of view. In this context, Pally (2000) writes:

> What is important to keep in mind is that amount of activity is the key factor in capturing the perceptual system. The patterns with the most activity 'win' (Calvin, 1996). Focused attention on a stimulus enhances activity in the cells processing that stimulus and not paying attention leads to decreased activity (Moran & Desimone, 1985). When attention enhances activity in a particular group of cells, the pattern of that group is more likely to be the dominant pattern and thus more likely to be what is perceived. (p. 32)

The implications of Pally's description are striking when, for example, in working with autistic children, as I do, one thinks of how the child's reliance on the use of autistic shapes and objects is literally creating a particular kind of brain, one that is minimally influenced by the interpersonal impact of other caring minds.

Keeping all these points of view in mind, I shall rely on the dictionary to define attention as "the capacity to focus upon an object in a voluntary or involuntary way; the capacity to become aware, select, and investigate particular phenomena ranging from the experience of bodily sensation up through complex mental events."

Attention in Psychoanalysis

The development of the capacity to choose to pay attention can be obstructed or facilitated by internal and external factors. The development of attention as a practical life skill must be considered as part of the overall development of the ego across the lifespan. A variety of special trainings can enhance and specialize attention. For example, consider the refined attention developed by a musician, a dancer, an athlete, or a chess player. Descriptions of Buddhist meditation masters would lead one to believe that attention as a capacity can be developed much more fully and variably than most people will ever realize experientially. As with other capacity-building activities, participation in psychoanalysis implicitly involves an ongoing training of attention.

Despite its practical and central place in treatment, attention is a mostly subterranean theme in the psychoanalytic literature, although evidence of its importance can be found in Freud's earliest work, including his 1895 *Project for a Scientific Psychology*. Among the writers who have explicitly explored the role of attention after Freud are Sullivan, Rappaport, Bion, Meltzer, Bromberg, and Boris. For now, I will not attempt to survey here the many ways that attention has been explored and developed within Freud's work or throughout the evolution of psychoanalysis. Bion's interest in this subject, however, merits a brief overview. In his paper "A Theory of Thinking" (1962), Bion describes a crossroads that emerges when one has the experience of frustration. Individuals with low frustration tolerance will attempt to evade their experiences, evacuating their distress through the phantasy of projective identification, while people who can tolerate frustration can begin to direct their attention to their experience in order to explore it and modify its frustrating qualities.

In *Learning from Experience*, Bion (1962) explicitly names attention as a factor in the work of alpha function. Later, he gives attention pride of place by creating column 4 on his Grid. Without going into a lengthy explanation of Bion's Grid, the entire horizontal axis can be viewed as a kind of process depiction of "the fate of attention."

One idea of Bion's that I find particularly important and want to describe in detail is that of reverie. Focusing on the process of reverie helps to both ground and enlarge the understanding of how essential the fate of attention is in the development of the capacity to learn from experience.

Reverie

The phenomenon of reverie, which Bion calls an expression of love, is a key variable influencing the quality of emotional experience and awareness. In its realization, the quality of the tangible presence of reverie, or its absence, is a crucial element in the overall growth of the mind.

In Bion's system of notation, the letter K stands for an openness to exploring, a willingness to "get to know." The presence of reverie makes "getting to know" possible. Minus K, on the other hand, is a category name he uses to denote the myriad ways that awareness of the impact of new emotional experiences can be obstructed. In the absence of adequate reverie, minus K impulses proliferate and can develop into unconscious habits that block or attack awareness of new experiences.

It's hard to pay attention when experiences are unfamiliar, difficult, or unpleasurable. Novelty increases the desire to pay attention if what is discovered brings pleasure. However, much of the time people unconsciously guard against the impact of new information, new ways of seeing, and new intensities of emotion, feeling, and desire. Bion emphasizes that each of us faces in his or her own way the unique challenge of building an apparatus for thinking that will allow us to continue to learn from experience over the course of a lifetime.

An apparatus for thinking begins to develop when a mother capable of reverie meets distress in a way that helps to make her infant's experience not only more emotionally tolerable but also potentially meaningful. What a mother consciously thinks about her infant's experience is significant, but it is important to keep in mind that reverie is a largely intuitive and unconscious process in terms of the mother's receptivity and imagination.

Bion asks the question: What does the mother's mind do for the infant in distress? Something helps the experience of raw emotional distress become an opportunity to evolve in the direction of discovering meaning. Bion says this something that helps is called "alpha function." The discovery of meaning depends upon the mother's ability to use her mind, including her attention, intuition, and imagination (all factors, I believe, in her alpha function) to receive and contain her infant's distress (the beta elements) and to transform that distress emotionally.

The capacity to pay attention, then, requires the availability of reverie. A mother's reverie sponsors a gradual awakening of the infant's subjective experience. Bion (1962) writes that a mother's capacity for reverie "is the receptor organ for the infant's harvest of self-sensation" (p. 116).

He suggests that the infant's "rudimentary consciousness" is unprepared on its own to deal with the experience of having experiences. Mother's reverie plays a protective and constructive role in modulating the infant's immersion in states of intense emotion and turbulent new experiences. Without access to reverie, the danger is that the infant will feel too much. An infant trapped in distress has no incentive to explore that experience, to tune into it and turn toward it, to tolerate it and to pay attention, or to allow awareness of the experience to build and evolve.

Listening to Yourself Listening

The psychoanalyst James Grotstein tells the story that one day while in analysis with Wilfred Bion he asked Bion, "Have I understood your interpretation correctly?" According to Grotstein Bion replied, "Don't listen to me, listen to yourself listening to me" (Grotstein, personal communication, 2004). I return to this advice repeatedly. I find it useful to practice creatively splitting my attention in order to learn how to listen to myself listening to another. I regard this way of listening as an element in the function of reverie. Listening to myself listening to another organizes attention over a widened field of experience.

Here is an ordinary example of the difficulty of being in a state of reverie with a disturbed patient.

Several years ago I worked with a woman whom I will call Maggie. Getting to know Maggie exposed me to confusing, contradictory, and seemingly exaggerated bits and pieces of experience. These bits and pieces multiplied from session to session, creating a dizzying atmosphere. Maggie had a sarcastic, biting wit, but she also expressed moments of genuine, almost innocent joy. Sometimes the bizarreness of her delusions intimidated me. The violence of the sadomasochism that emerged in the transference was at times horrifying. Sometimes Maggie spoke of her fading hope and lost ambitions in a way that palpably radiated another kind of pain. The intensity of her struggle to accept her own experience felt heartbreaking. This was especially true as Maggie approached describing a kind of black hole of despair and then seemed to teeter on the edge of rejecting the whole human species in bouts of ferocious cynicism, only to recover and days later speak with genuine appreciation of some moment that, as she put it, made her feel human again.

It was hard to pay attention to Maggie and to listen to myself listening to her at the same time. Sometimes the force of her communications disabled my attention and I felt a confusion bordering on panic. At other times, particularly in relation to her delusions, it was as if my attention was almost paralyzed by her shocking conviction about what seemed to her obvious facts and what seemed to me wild, nightmarish improbabilities. I experienced numerous instances of not being able to process rapidly enough the shame, disgust, and horror that I felt filled up with. These intensities were registered in my body and left me vulnerable to my own attacking fears and doubts, which intruded upon my consciousness and sometimes threatened to hijack my attention.

There were other things, too, that in a more subtle way had a strong effect on the deployment of my attention. Maggie's voice could be sweet and content, childlike and helpless, gruff and decaying, or sour and even poisonously mocking. The shifting quality of Maggie's voice often carried an enormous but elusive violence within it. Sometimes I had powerful somatic reactions, both during the meetings and sometimes hours afterward. Once I had terrible nightmares that I intuitively linked to our work together. These experiences helped me to appreciate how concretely embodied Bion conceives the operation of *beta elements* to be.

It is important, I think, to feel into and appreciate the atmosphere of catastrophe at the level of sensation that can accompany one's experience when attention and reflective consciousness are becoming overwhelmed. Nobody wants to pay attention when exposed to confusion, distress, or the fear of overwhelming pain, whether mental or physical. Yet this willingness to pay attention, to get to know the quality and texture of an experience, is precisely what Bion says can gradually help to contain and transform experience.

When we can face our own fears, when we can open up to honestly accept the suffering that is so vividly present, we can discover a deep feeling of human resonance and even begin to appreciate a native creativity that some people like Maggie can improbably initiate us into welcoming. So much of daily life is designed to defend against the rawness of experience. Working with people like Maggie can open up whole new channels of attention and perception.

The Fate of Attention

Our habits of attention are organized in our earliest experiences and relationships. Ordinarily an infant comes into the world prepared to pay attention, specifically to the presence of its mother. The experience of attention is negotiated unconsciously through the facilitating atmosphere of reverie established in numerous "proto conversations" (Trevarthen) and interactions between a mother and her infant unfolding over time.

A mother capable of reverie naturally woos her infant's attention beyond a merely concrete, sensation-dominated experience as she unconsciously stimulates in her infant the preconception of psychic reality. If all goes well, over time the infant experiences a dawning intuition of the enigma of his own mind as well as the mind of another.

The development of the capacity for attention depends upon the adequate establishment of what Bion named a container–contained relationship. It is also, I infer, deeply linked to what Meltzer has named the "aesthetic conflict," which involves the infant's capacity to tolerate the intense impact of beauty and the mystery of mother's subjective presence.

These complex, prereflective, affectively intense experiences are either mediated by mother's reverie or, in its absence, may become the source of a bombardment of impressions, leading to anxiety, depression, or persecution. Unbearable impinging experience causes, I believe, the infant's evolving proto-attentional capacities to be split off, withdrawn, or even to collapse.

Here we must consider many different kinds of risk factors, among them the inborn variables of hypersensitivity and hyperirritability (and their opposites) that Grotstein has described as critical vulnerabilities in the etiology of disorders of primitive mental states. Fetal disturbances and difficulty in the birth process may also have lasting negative impacts, not only on overall growth and attachment but also specifically on the capacity to turn toward and seek out the object. Early experiences of sensory overwhelm and distress can become equated with the presence of the mother or other caretaker, leading the nascent self to withdraw in aversion from contact with others. In states of this kind, the child develops a disincentive to attend to others and sometimes even to his or her own sense of embodiment.

Something?
this
orig...

Situations involving profound maternal depression, or a mother's un-
contained psychotic anxieties, or occurrences of overt trauma and neglect
are some of the many other potentially important variables that lead to
early withdrawal from object seeking and to the kind of omnipotent
survival activities described by Symington (see Chapter 5). In such situations, attention is captured in an unconscious fear of catastrophe rather
than being free to make contact and explore emotional experience.

Attention and Autism

Work with children with autistic features brings anomalies of attention
to the foreground. Engaging children with features of this kind requires
both patience and sensitive activity on the part of the analyst. Helping a
child move from captured attention to the ability to share attention is a
crucial part of the process of building an apparatus for thinking and for
sponsoring the capacity to learn from experience.

I am impressed, in our initial meetings, by the way autistic children fail to acknowledge my presence and how their attention appears
trapped in deeply idiosyncratic activities. Their attention is captured or
fixed, not only by the creation of autistic shapes or objects, as described
by Frances Tustin, but also in sensation-dominated scenes, ideas, images, and scenarios. Usually such worlds remain hidden and private.
Psychoanalysis creates the conditions to reveal, explore, and share these
secret, sensation-dominated countries of the mind.

Tustin emphasizes the use of autistic defenses to guard against the
impact of the catastrophic awareness of premature separation. She considered the sensation-dominated use of autistic objects and shapes to be
largely mindless. The children I have gotten to know, diagnosed with
autism or Asperger's at the University of Washington, appear to experience their attention in other ways, too. They are children who the careful
observer might say are "elsewhere" rather than mindless.

While sensation dominated, these children, given an adequate therapeutic setting, show themselves to be involved in complicated and often
very disturbing private emotional scenarios. These private scenarios seem
to dominate at least a portion of their attention. I find that although
it appears that their attention is totally captured, on closer observation

another quantity of attention, as it were, is unemployed, waiting in the wings, potentially available to be harnessed if sensitively acknowledged. Part of the difficulty in reaching such children involves the complicated challenge of learning to recognize and harness moments of initiative and contact that are sometimes present in the child's behavior or intention but remain undetected or unrecognized.

Why is it so hard to make contact with these children? Some of the child's hidden worlds seem more emotionally real to the child than the interpersonal worlds of family, school, and community. As the autistic child ages, the pressures to communicate and comply with the expectations of the interpersonal world increase. Living, as it were, in the virtual world makes fewer conscious demands on the child while the interpersonal world grows more baffling and intimidating. I think that for many children there is a deep confusion as the virtual world bleeds into the interpersonal world, and vice versa. Evidence of this confusion can often be seen in both violent tantrums and massive withdrawal from others. It is crucial in therapy to help the child to begin to differentiate between psychic reality and the external world so that she can choose how to direct attention.

Using Meltzer's metaphor, when the tiller of attention is somehow stuck it is difficult to steer a flexible course. In order to communicate with such children, you must first discover what has captured the child's attention. Then, gradually, you can learn how to get and to keep the child's attention in order to eventually establish what Frances Tustin (1986) calls "a rhythm of safety." Tustin emphasizes that the discovery of the rhythm of safety is "an everyday miracle" because it involves the movement from isolated attention to "shared experience." The rhythm of safety involves a rhythm of *interaction*, which is the creation of two embodied minds meeting (p. 274).

I have been surprised, in some cases, at how quickly I can establish a relationship, however tentative and shallow, with some children. When they finally make contact with a containing mind capable of reverie I have witnessed what I would describe as the emergence of a highly charged internal drama that I shall call the *background of catastrophe*. The background of catastrophe emerges in the infantile transference as the child begins to express herself by discovering how to play in the presence of another.

Several elements go into the creation of the configuration I am calling a background of catastrophe. They seem to include the pragmatic problems of hypersensitivity and sensory integration, as well as evidence of an internal projective identification rejecting object (Bion's obstructive object), entrenched splitting of the primitive masculine and feminine qualities of the self, and overwhelming emotional intensity. All these elements, taken together, create enormous obstacles to seeking the other, communicating, and sharing experience. It is the background of catastrophe that captures the child attention, paradoxically, because it is both overwhelming, and at the same time demanding attention so as to be dreamt, symbolized, and communicated.

Shared Attention

When mother and infant, or analyst and patient, can *share* emotional experiences, attention develops freely along the lines of awareness of self, awareness of other, and the dawning awareness of the importance of the relationship between self and other. Alvarez and Furgiuele (1997) write:

> One could speculate that the baby's paying attention to two objects at once (that is, to mother's background interest and the new object's foreground magnetism) may be facilitated by mother's ability to wait for the return of baby's attention to her – that is by acceptance of his two-trackedness. He learns to accept her interest in other objects – father, siblings, household chores, the telephone – but she, too, learns to accept and respect his curiosity in things and people other than herself. (p. 128)

This developing capacity for sharing attention is an important background quality necessary for emotional contact and ultimately for the capacity for self-reflection. Over time the experiences of *sharing attention* evolve. Attention to self, attention to the other, and attention to the link between self and other make a quantum leap in complexity when it is extended to include other figures in the field. Each of these differentiating forms of awareness becomes part of what I picture as an unconscious field of attention. The field of attention is, I believe, an important facet of what Grotstein has called "the background presence of primary identification." Grotstein (2000) writes:

> I see human infants as experiencing themselves as incompletely separated from a mythical object behind them, their background presence, their object of tradition, which rears them and sends them forth....
>
> This Background Presence evolves from being a co-participant in the mysterious oneness of primary identification to being a released and backwardly departing soul or spirit of comforting protection.... All this takes place as infants accept separation and find the confidence to use their epistemophilic capacities (designated as K by Bion) in conjunction with libidinal organization (Bion's L) and their inherent, undifferentiated defense organization.... *The Background Presence helps to coordinate the K, L, and H focus on all objects of scrutiny so that the sense organs can individually and collectively categorize and conceptualize strange and separate objects to make them familiar.* (pp. 17–18, emphasis added)

Grotstein seems to suggest that the infant, relying upon the background presence, will coordinate and organize its attention in order to give significance to its gradually expanding construction of reality.

I posit the importance in ordinary development of an ever-expanding field of attention as part of what sponsors the capacity to learn from experience. The field of attention is, like Bion's model of the contact barrier, made up of a constant accumulation of alpha elements in the transformation from beta → alpha. The field of attention is strengthened by the auxiliary alpha function from other generous minds willing to help process the impact of experience. There are always pockets of beta elements untouched by alpha function because there is never enough alpha function. But, in a good-enough situation, I imagine there is a steady expansion of the field of attention to reclaim some of the unmentalized aspects of personal experience as well as to meet new experience in a spirit of getting-to-know.

New experiences transform the field of attention as part of a learning process that differentiates and structures awareness in the evolving categories of *my* attention, *your* attention, *our* attention, *others'* attention, and the complex awareness of attention taking itself as an object of interest. Consider, if you will, how differently experience feels and seems when different kinds of attention can be investigated freely.

These qualities are realized within a family context through the parents' capacity to welcome the infant's and the child's projective identifications as meaningful forms of communication. When the infant can experience her mother or father or optimally the parental couple as *projective identification welcoming objects*, she gains a sense of confidence in allowing and seeking emotional experiences. The realization and continuing evolution of *internal* projective identification welcoming objects is sponsored by an internalization of what James Gooch has called "robust parental reverie" (Gooch, 2002). Experience augmented by such reverie can extend attention beyond concern with survival or compliant adaptation into explorations of being, belonging, creating, and discovering. Such experiences are then shared with other live and passionate subjects.

In cases of trauma or deprivation, this field of attention can be stunted, depleted, torn, or, in the worst cases, it may barely begin to exist at all. Grotstein (2000) writes:

> The sense of continuity is experienced as having been lost or never formed, and in its place is a series of fearful discontinuities forever isolated and estranged from each other. This phenomenon emerges from the painful, primal, pathological splitting of the personality, in contrast to normal, discriminating splitting, and is descended from that primal awareness of being split off from the primal object. It can be spatially visualized *as turning one's back on awareness in lieu of accepting it.* (pp. 19–20, emphasis added)

Our styles of attending, then, are clues to our habits of suffering. Our analytic task involves, I believe, becoming more conscious of our styles of attending and their deep infantile roots. It is beyond the scope of this chapter to extend this exploration into the structuring role of attention in the Oedipus scene and the discovery of mental space and what Britton has called "triangular space." Attention, I believe, must be considered a critical variable in these dynamic evolving structures of the mind.

Toward a Deepening Reverie

My work has motivated me to reflect upon my own states of mind and how I use myself as an instrument, for better or worse, in the psychoanalytic process. Over time I have become increasingly interested in the difficult-to-describe experience of the analyst's use of the self when listening to himself listening to another. I am committed to continuing to explore this area with the goal in mind of deepening my capacity for reverie. Paying attention to attention is one factor in the deepening function of reverie.

In "Recommendations for Physicians on the Psychoanalytic Method of Treatment," Freud (1912) famously writes:

> The technique ... is a very simple one. It disclaims the use of any special aids ... and simply consists in making no effort to concentrate the attention on anything in particular, and in maintaining in regard to all that one hears the same measure of calm, quiet attentiveness – 'of evenly hovering attention'.... All conscious exertion is to be withheld from the capacity for attention, and one's 'unconscious memory' is to be given full play; or to express it in terms of technique, pure and simple: One has simply to listen and not to trouble to keep in mind anything in particular. (pp. 324–25)

Why did Freud advocate this particular way of working? He explains:

> What one achieves in this way will be sufficient for all requirements during the treatment. Those elements of the material which have a connection with one another will be at the conscious disposal of the physician; the rest, as yet unconnected, chaotic and indistinguishable, seems at first to disappear, but rises readily into recollection as soon as the patient brings something further to which it is related, and by which it can be developed. (p. 325)

Freud's faith in this special form of effortless listening was provocatively reformulated, many years later, by Bion. Bion's emphasis on the importance of eschewing memory, desire, and understanding conveys, I believe, important instructions designed to define the conditions for increasing the possibility of realizing a deeper form of reverie.

Memory and desire are described by Bion as resistances to intuition and as defenses against the turbulence of the awareness of the evolution of O. In ordinary daily experience we are constantly moving, consciously and unconsciously, between aspects of memory and desire in our thoughts, feelings, ideas, and fantasies. Memory, desire, and anticipation easily capture our attention and give us the illusion of knowledge. We can easily move from getting to know to the reified illusion of knowing, a natural misrepresentation of a deeper process according to Bion.

Reverie, like contact with our dream life, is probably a natural capacity available in each of us to a greater or lesser degree. Deepening reverie, on the other hand, requires discipline, practice, and courage to begin to realize. One might say that cultivating deepening reverie requires self-consciously "training the mind." It is not clear what the limits of this form of experience might be for any particular individual.

Ordinary reverie is part of the K system, indicating willingness to get-to-know an experience. Deepening reverie is another way, I suggest, of naming and elaborating what Bion calls "an act of faith." An act of faith belongs to the O system. Bion (1970) writes:

> Before interpretations of hallucination can be given ... it is necessary that the analyst undergoes in his own personality the transformation O → K. By eschewing memories, desires, and the operations of memory he can approach the domain of hallucinosis and of the 'acts of faith' by which alone he can become at one with his patients' hallucinations and so effect transformations O → K. (p. 36)

For the psychoanalyst, consciousness and attention pose practical problems. Attention cannot be addressed until one begins to describe what the analyst is supposed to attend to. In differentiating the physician from the analyst, Bion proposes the idea of "intuiting" as the equivalent, in the domain of psychic reality, of seeing, touching, tasting, smelling, and hearing. One must somehow be able to register information from one's own psychic reality and attend to it in order to perceive an evolution sponsored by the impact of being with a particular patient at a particular moment in a particular session. Bion is explicit about this. In *Attention and Interpretation* (1970), he writes:

> The analyst must focus his attention on O, the unknown and un-knowable. The success of psycho-analysis depends on the maintenance of a psycho-analytic point of view; the point of view is the psycho-analytic vertex; the psycho-analytic vertex is O. With this the analyst cannot be identified: he must be it. (p. 27)

How can you take the unknown or unknowable as an object of attention? Put simply, you cannot: O cannot be made into an object. The practical problem is to find a way to deploy your attention in the service of intuiting and becoming at-one with O. This task is fostered, according to Bion, through a negative strategy of disciplining memory, desire, and understanding, as well as learning to eschew reliance on sense impressions as orienting coordinates. This ambitious discipline is designed to be a practical aid to fostering observation of another kind of experience. One aims to free attention and consciousness in order to increase the chances of being able to register the intangible evolution of O. The problem that then follows is how to represent and communicate what one intuits in the transformation O → K. Ultimately Bion will assert that intuition is the tool for psychoanalytic observation, and the capacity to welcome thoughts in search of a thinker will define his mature definition of the psychoanalyst's task.

Clinical Vignette

To ground these ideas in personal experience, I shall offer a condensed vignette from the continuing treatment of an eight-year-old whom I will call Stuart. Stuart was diagnosed with autism at the University of Washington. When I met him, Stuart's symptoms included violent tantrums, during which he would smear his feces on the walls of his house and intentionally urinate on his parents' bed. He also sometimes experienced spasms of flapping his hands back and forth in front of his face, hitting his face, biting his tongue, squealing, and screaming.

Stuart was born at thirty weeks. He was in an incubator for seven and a half weeks, and on ventilators and tube-fed for the same period of time. Stuart never breast fed. His mother reports that as a baby he constantly vomited, although he showed adequate weight gain. He has had sleep problems all his life, including occasional night terrors. Additionally, Stuart has suffered from asthma and chronic ear infections.

Stuart is a strikingly handsome boy. He is thin but strongly built. He is very intelligent although his communications were initially sparse verbally. Stuart is also very musical in a primitive way. He sings, hums, whimpers, and grunts throughout his sessions. I will share part of the story of Stuart's emergence in his first year of treatment and show why I believe an atmosphere of deepening reverie was crucial to making contact with an infantile aspect of the transference.

Early in our work Stuart discovered a game he called "resting." He would come in, lie on my couch, and, in a mournful voice would say "I just need to rest." I realized quickly that there was nothing to talk about, that I should just sit in my chair and attentively watch over him.

Stuart would burrow into the back of the couch, face to the pillows, tucked in on himself. He would cover himself completely with the afghan on the back of the couch. He would sometimes shudder and convulse. He would make the most pathetic whimpering sounds like a small animal.

I felt that I must not try to explain too early these phenomena nor speak out loud the emotionally intense narrative that was gradually forming in my mind. I thought it was crucial that I allow a space within me to register and reflect upon this experience rather than rushing to reply to it.

I had the intuition that Stuart was, as Winnicott might say, gathering the trauma in and trying to master it within the sphere of his own omnipotent experience, perhaps trying to discover and feel a certain form of facilitating omnipotent illusion. I also felt, simultaneously, that Stuart was "making a scene" and that I needed to welcome it in order to become an audience who might comprehend something he was trying unconsciously to express.

I felt there might be a double kind of process happening as this scenario unfolded over several sessions. As I sat with Stuart, who I will remind you was largely silent except for his sporadic whimpers, I wondered to myself, Is he somehow trying to unconsciously master the trauma of his earliest life in the incubator? In my reverie I felt increasingly open to feelings of being without any boundaries, terrified, horribly exposed, and vulnerable to an unseen, unformed menace.

I sensed what felt to me like a potentially overpowering and unspeakable existential grief as Stuart's whimpers turned slowly into bits of melody and partial songs. I had the terrible feeling of not knowing what Stuart's behavior was meant to convey, only that it was meaningful and that I must tolerate not knowing the meaning of it until something became more obvious to me.

Gradually I realized we were existing in a realm more easily understood as an animal one. If I were an animal parent I might have picked him up and carried him to a nest or protected space and groomed him by licking him to help him be soothed or comforted.

I felt as if I were both at-one with the premature infant state and at the same time a parent observing something impossible to fathom. I had glimpses of what it might be like to cling to a sense of life, to live, as it were, next door to death. My consciousness and attention were split between an imaginative involvement with an infantile catastrophe, and a careful observation of Stuart's behavior, as well as my own reactions to it. I was determined *not* to put any of this into words between us. In my reverie I protected a space for these experiences to develop and feel real before deciding whether or how to share them. I felt I could not be sure of any of my impressions. Yet they also had a profound emotional reality for me.

It is important to know that the resting game took place for only portions of a session and that Stuart did not play this game in every session. It does seem linked to his awareness of separation and a growing sense of his own separateness.

One day, while I was again observing his resting game, Stuart looked up at me from under the blankets. He made a very long sustained eye contact with me. His gaze had an intense impact on me and I felt, now, that it was as if he were asking for me to speak to him about this experience. Before, when he was completely under the cover of the afghan, I could not speak to him without intruding. This time there seemed to be an invitation to share my experience with him.

With both trepidation and conviction I said to Stuart: "What is going through my mind is a story, a very emotional story, about a tiny baby. I have been thinking about this for a long time. I think about you as a tiny baby, right after you were born from your mother's tummy. You were so tiny and it was too early to come out. I wonder now, when you are trying to rest, if you are trying to start over, trying to find an atmosphere where there is not so much worry all around you, and you can feel welcomed into the world in a new way."

Stuart seemed to listen to me very carefully. He got up off the couch and went to my toy area and took the toys out of a small box made of clear plastic. He brought the box to the center of the room. He then tried to step into the box, which was much too small for him. Then he lay down on the ground in a fetal position on his side and pressed his face into the box so that he was looking at me through the clear plastic.

I said: "Now you are showing me the tiny baby you once were who lived in an incubator and looked at others through the barrier of the walls of that box. This happened so long ago and yet it feels now as if it were right now too. That tiny lost baby is trying to be found right now by me and by you."

Stuart lay on the ground for some time, mewing. I said that he was trying to orient himself and have a sense of safety by creating a series of sounds to contain himself.

Stuart said: "It's okay, Jeff. I understand. Really I do."

I thought he might be feeling a need to reassure me—but I also felt he was saying that he valued what I was saying and was working on it privately inside himself.

I believe that this experience is an example of risking, of allowing a deepening reverie to emerge both within myself, by listening to myself listening to Stuart, and between Stuart and me. The experience of reverie becomes part of the shared field of experience where we can both attend to a mysterious emotional evolution that neither of us could predict might emerge. This kind of process, it seems to me, is what allows for the deepening symbolization that is part of the heart of how psychoanalysis works as a form of therapy.

Concluding Thoughts

The psychoanalyst Harold Boris (1993), a keen student of Bion, writes:

> To the extent that the rudimentary ability to volitionally deploy our attention gains in scope, by dint of practice and the development of brainpower, our mind gains proportionate freedom from what was previously thrust upon it. We can turn away, though only—forever—by turning elsewhere. (p. 49)

What do we seek? What do we avoid? Where does our attention lead us? How lost do we become in split-off states of mind? What do we believe is possible and impossible? With awareness, one can begin to observe habits of aversion to negative emotions as well as habits of seeking to prolong or possess positive experiences. We often try (unconsciously) to dominate and control experiences through the use of attention, and, as Sullivan observed, through the use of selective inattention (and denial). Can one stay with curiosity and desire, love or hate, rather than turning away from experience when turbulence or conflict looms? Can one explore the emergence of a feeling rather than possessively or domineeringly intruding into the object that stimulates it? Finally, do we have the courage to attend to those moments of intuition, to the thought in search of a thinker?

We turn toward our suffering or we turn away, and this choice, conscious as well as unconscious, is a crucial ingredient in our own evolving sense of identity. I believe we can become more skillful at paying attention to attention, and in doing so we can gather wisdom from the simple act of mindfully attending to our dreams and feelings, and the intuitions generated by deepening contact with everyday life.

CHAPTER NINE

Listening to Yourself
Listening to Another

N THIS CHAPTER, I OFFER SOME THOUGHTS ON REVERIE.
I explore the relationship between reverie and a process called listening to yourself listening to another. I have neither tried to survey here the voluminous literature on psychoanalytic listening nor the
equally relevant area of countertransference. Instead, my intention is to
make a personal statement based upon my evolving experience as a psychoanalyst, drawing mainly on the ideas of Wilfred Bion and of analysts
inspired by Bion's work.

James Grotstein tells the story that, while in analysis with Bion, he
asked Bion one day, "Have I understood your interpretation correctly?"
According to Grotstein (personal communication, 2004), Bion replied
"Don't listen to me, listen to yourself listening to me." I have repeatedly
returned to this advice. It makes sense that if we only listen to the other
we will miss a large part of the experience—that is, our own. I have
found that a different kind of experience, the potential for reverie, opens
up when you are encouraged to listen to yourself listening to the other.

Reverie

In a Bionian model of development, the infant's evolving capacity for
experiencing emotion is crucial in the overall growth of her mind. Bion
(1962) introduced the idea of reverie as a key variable influencing the
quality of experience between a mother and her infant. Reverie can
be described as a mother's capacity to register her infant's distress, reflect upon it, and reply to it. A mother capable of reverie meets distress,

and all of her infant's nascent emotional states, in a way that helps to make her infant's experience not only more tolerable but also potentially meaningful.

This Bionian model highlights a mother's unconscious capacity to welcome her infant's projective identifications as a primitive form of communication. Put more plainly, in understanding that her infant is experiencing some form of pain, a mother naturally attempts to help her infant move from distress to comfort, and does so repeatedly.

She does this by providing a mental function (Bion calls it *alpha function*) that accompanies her physical holding, soothing, and caring for her baby. This mental function, when sufficiently robust, creates a discernible atmosphere marked by the tangible presence of care, imagination, and mindfulness. The interest generated by this emotional atmosphere creates a novel experience strong enough to coexist with the infant's sensations of pain and distress. The infant's attention is thus attracted by this atmosphere of mindfulness, and she is then freer to be repeatedly wooed into a deepening emotional relationship with her mother.

In essence, we can say that the presence of reverie creates the possibility of an unconscious choice, the possibility of an emotional transformation that can be sought after. In the absence of reverie, the infant is in danger of becoming lost in the concreteness of its distress, having its entire attention captured by its pain.

Faith in the reliability of a primal transformation from distress to comfort punctuates the infant's evolving relationship to mother and sponsors the child's sense of a mysterious dawning awareness of her mother's mind. Christopher Bollas, inspired by both Winnicott and Bion, has written beautifully about what he calls "the maternal idiom" and its impact not only on development but also on the structure of the infant's unconscious sense of identity. Whatever we call it, this nascent awareness of the qualities of the sensibility of the other becomes part of the early unconscious emotional floor of experience.

For Bion, proto-awareness of a subjective register of experience is a critical early realization. This recognition involves a slowly dawning domain of significance that begins to accrue along with the organizing of sensation and perception. Although for the infant these early realizations are presymbolic, intersubjective experience expands through the expression of the mother's capacity for reverie and the infant's capacity to receive it. Such a situation creates the conditions for the psychological birth of the infant and further facilitates the growth of the infant's own realization of psychic reality.

Reverie can be contrasted with mindlessness, as well as with psychic deadness. It is common, I think, for a parent to offer competent, concrete, loving care for an infant while not recognizing the importance of the domain of subjectivity or the dawning psychic reality in their very young child. While reverie gradually helps to make the differentiation of psychic experiences possible, the absence of such mindfulness leaves the infant's psychic experience potentially underdeveloped and undifferentiated.

When reverie is present, sensation spreads out into myriad forms of emotional aliveness. When reverie is absent, sensation can be felt as an impingement, even as a bombardment, and in extreme cases, the source of psychic catastrophe. The provision of reverie makes awareness of experience possible while its absence can lead, according to Bion, to an enforced splitting that forecloses the development and realization of a unique and separate awareness of having a mind of one's own.

The infant's experience in a negative scenario of this kind can be described as being trapped in a concrete dimension of two-dimensional perception. In such a state, there is a relentless focus upon materialistic solutions that can continue on as a style of relating to experience well into later life. As the child ages, the experience of emotion feels as if it were visited upon the subject from outside the body, and contact with emotion brings a crisis of fear, including the fear of death, because emotions are felt to be foreign, threatening, and explosive. This naturally leads to a suspicion, and even hatred, of emotion. One can often observe the presence of a profound anti-emotional attitude as a tenacious way of surviving and being in the world.

James Grotstein describes how a mother's capacity for reverie helps to create the container function that Bion stresses is a precursor to the development of the capacity for thinking. Grotstein (1980) writes:

Bion's conception of the container... is more like that of a prism which refracts the monochromatic scream of the infant into its

varying hues of the emotional color spectrum so as to differentiate them and, having sorted them out, act upon them individu-
ally and collectively. In so doing, the container is not merely a
passive function of flexibility or elasticity but is rather one of
transformation of the infant's monochromatic screams into data
of mental significance which can and should be acted upon by the
maternal container. (p. 486)

When a mother cannot adequately offer this containing function or
when a baby cannot reliably make use of it, a baby can feel abandoned to
its distress, which, when amplified by other additional factors, becomes
a situation that Bion describes as terminating in "nameless dread."

In situations of sustained neglect or deprivation, the absence of reverie can become the presence of intense, ego-destructive experiences for
the infant. As a consequence, the presence of reverie and what it implies
for how the mind grows or fails to grow is enormous. Unmodified mental pain leads, according to Bion, to a hatred of emotion and finally to a
hatred of experience of any kind.

Reverie, in this way of thinking, then, is also a crucial variable in the
creation of an analytic process that promotes therapeutic action through
learning from experience. The "alpha function" of the analyst is a necessary stimulus for the patient, encouraging a process of transformation
that makes it possible to experience that which could not be tolerated or
approached before. In this model, change is conceptualized not as cure
but as the development of new capacities of self that sponsor the growth
of an apparatus for thinking, feeling, and experiencing.

Reverie and the Parental Couple

What conditions make it possible to open up to new or painful experiences? Reverie is often thought about as dyadic in structure. Christopher
Bollas, who has significantly described the importance of the maternal
idiom and the transformational object, proffers a triangular structure
for experience that, to me, deepens the appreciation of reverie as a function that fosters the growth of a greater capacity for welcoming new
experiences.

Bollas (1999) describes differing orders of experience that can be pictured as elaborating an Oedipal structure. In them, functions or orders of experience (p. 37) are personified as a dreaming baby, a mother holding the dreaming baby in a state of primary maternal preoccupation, and a father guaranteeing the separateness of each participant. Father's role, in this model, helps to establish the space of communal language, culture, and the values of the wider outside world. Bollas's model draws on Freud, Klein, Winnicott, Bion, and Lacan, and proposes the coexistence in each mind of these three interdependent orders, each influencing and enhancing the others.

The theme of father as a necessary third, and as one toward whom mother can turn to break the magic spell of union with her infant, is important in many analytic schools of thought. James Gooch (2002), building on the work of Donald Meltzer and Frances Tustin, explicitly develops the role of father in the creation and expansion of the capacity for reverie.

Gooch has proposed a model of maternal reverie augmented by paternal reverie that expands the containing function through the couple's creative cooperative relationship. In Gooch's model, maternal reverie multiplied by paternal reverie creates parental reverie. Parental reverie is robust because it is the balanced combination of discipline and compassion found in both parents. Discipline is understood to mean the willingness to frustrate and set limits, even to cause pain when necessary, arising out of the spirit of protection and love. Compassion is understood as the ability not only to tolerate suffering but also to actively investigate it in order to lessen it and to learn from it. Discipline without compassion tends toward sadism, while compassion without discipline tends toward masochism. Gooch's ideal of the creative parental couple involves a mature bisexuality in each partner that strengthens each person's influence for the benefit of the growing baby, child, and family. In this scenario, the participants continue to expand their capacity for reverie over the course of the life span. Significantly, even when the interpersonal provision of such reverie cannot actually be realized in one's family, the self that is capable of recognizing and taking in the bits and pieces of reverie gleaned from daily life can sometimes use these to realize and expand such an inner couple. This constitutes, from a post-Kleinian point of view, something close to the central reason for doing analysis. Analytic work, like dream life itself, may be capable of sponsoring symbolic realizations that lead to the recognition and growth of an internal couple capable of sustaining and expanding an attitude of deepening reverie that can transform the self's sense of identity and its capacity for learning.

Paying Attention

How do we know what to listen to when listening to a patient? What attracts our attention? What are we averse to? What do we fail to notice, or even deny unconsciously? Is it possible to listen to ourselves while at the same time listening to another? James Gooch once shared this metaphor with me. Gooch invites you to think of your attention as if it were a large fishing net. He says that you can cast your attention like a net into the sea of the session and go trawling for emotion. He speaks of this as letting the net drift and sink, and then from time to time hauling it in to see what you have gathered. He suggests that it is this harvest of attention that allows you to examine the various bits of emotion and experience that are discovered in the session.

It is through investigating the harvest of attention that the experience of analysis continues to evolve in an intimate, here-and-now fashion. Gradually analyst and patient become partners in this reflective cooperative process. As reverie evolves through exploration, each partner takes an interest in the dialectical evolution of what their separate and shared attention gathers.

Bion famously said that when two personalities meet an emotional storm is created. Bion also emphasized how far we go out of our way not to meet each other. So there is a basic question at the heart of every session: "Who is this other human being and how will I come to know about their experience today?" (Franco Scabbiolo, personal communication).

I remember, for example, working with a man who had spent several years in prison for a violent assault. One day he came to his session with his head shaved. Although I was already frightened of him at times, on this particular day I felt an immediate dread. The moment he walked into my office the atmosphere felt thick and electric. Somehow it was as if all the history of violence in his experience became immediate and tangible in the fact of his now bald head.

He told me about his sleepless night and described the pleasure he took in impulsively shaving his head—which, he said, changed his state of mind and allowed him to go to sleep. Suddenly he was a vivid, living, breathing, suffering body in front of me. All the abstraction cluttering my mind drained away. The stories he'd told me took on sharp new immediacy. His shaven head was like a fire alarm. Now I began to investigate a not very hidden world, a world I had not yet been willing or able to extend my capacity for reverie toward.

In our work, we strive to understand the person as an experiencing human subject, not as a set of symptoms, defenses, conflicts, and transferences. The challenge is to extend reverie into places where it may never have been experienced or welcomed before. This is a shared task, not just a task of the analyst or the patient alone.

Two Minds Finding Each Other: Intersubjectivity

Although it is beyond the scope of this chapter to describe in detail, I want to note the way that intrapsychic and interpersonal experience inform and influence each other. The idea of listening to yourself listening to another implies the potential exploration of a third realm of experience. The intersubjective realm encompasses the complex process by and during which two minds find and know each other. In experiences of this kind a third entity is created. This entity has been given many different names depending upon the theorists you prefer. Here, I want to emphasize the importance of attention to the *emotional field* arising between analyst and analysand. The way we conceptualize this interpenetration of experience seems to make a great deal of difference in the way we register, reflect, and reply to the other.

This process also touches on the long-standing question of how an infant internalizes the mother's reverie or alpha function. While the question is to some degree complicated by the idea of the infant's need to internalize a good object, what Bion highlights is not the qualities of the object alone, but the qualities of the link—the nature of the relationship between self and object. This is an important transformation of perspective because it places a different emphasis on the fate of attention. In a good-enough situation, where reverie has been adequate, what is internalized, in Grotstein's important phrasing, is "the legacy of the influence of the object, not the object itself" (Grotstein, personal communication).

In the analytic context, Thomas Ogden (1999) has written elegantly on this area and gives a name to this evolving experience of shared attention. He calls it "the analytic third." He writes:

> This third subject stands in dialectical tension with the separate individual subjectivities of analyst and analysand in such a way that the individual subjectivities and the third create, negate, and preserve each other.... Each experiences the analytic third in the context of his own separate personality system, his own particular ways of layering and linking conscious and unconscious aspects of experience, his own ways of experiencing and integrating bodily sensations, the unique history and development of his external and internal object relations, and so on. In short, the analytic third is not a single event experienced identically by two people; it is an unconscious, asymmetrical co-creation of analyst and analysand which has a powerful structuring influence on the analytic relationship. (unpaginated)

In this formulation, then, reverie belongs not only to the mother or to the therapist. Reverie becomes a factor in the deepening of all communication and sponsors the possibility of creative discovery in the analytic couple.

The Capacity for Observation

Toward the end of his life, the psychoanalyst Donald Meltzer (2005) had this to say about observation:

> The first step is to recognize that the state of "observation" is essentially a resting state. Second, that it is also a state of heightened vigilance. I compare it with waiting in the dark for the deer, grazing at night, seen by their flashing white tails. This nocturnal vigilance is on the alert for movement of the quarry, part-object

minimal movements which with patience form a pattern of incipient meaning "cast before". This catching of the incipient meaning cast before is a function of receptive imagination—"open to the possible", unconcerned with probability. Being rich in suspense, it is necessarily fatiguing, even exhausting. However, it is a poetry generator. (p. 182)

What are some of the qualities that sponsor this "resting state" and make observation possible?

In a Bionian model of development, one must become ever more capable of welcoming projective identifications as meaningful signals of incipient emotional experience. The welcoming of these flashes of intuition helps expand what Bion called a container–contained relationship. Being a containing object with reverie and alpha function is complex, in that one must register and reflect upon not only the communications of the other, but also what is evoked within oneself by the impact of the other.

In other words, I need to become a keen observer of my own capacity to welcome spontaneous psychic impressions generated in the moment-to-moment encounter with my patient. I need to realize and expand an open relationship not only with my patient but also specifically with myself, as well as to my own process of accepting or rejecting emergent emotional experience. This begins, according to Meltzer, with a state of "heightened vigilance," characterized by the ability to detect, register, tolerate, attend to, investigate, and imaginatively elaborate what Meltzer calls "part-object minimal movements."

We cannot free ourselves from our own filters of perception, nor should we try to. There is no privileged stance for observation. We see the world in certain ways based largely upon our histories and the various conflicts and compromises that make up who we are becoming. We make meaning based upon those unconscious realities structured by the template of our own internal object relations. It does no good to say that our capacity for observation is contaminated by our personal experience. We have only personal experience to reply with.

I strive to work with that which becomes conscious, and then, taking the next step, to reflectively investigate the experience of having an experience. As part of this investigation, I consider the context within which my experience arises, that is, the psychoanalytic setting with a particular patient during a particular sequence of emotional moments.

I notice the experience of contact or lack of contact, both with the patient and also with my own psychic reality. Observation can spur me to try to notice the meanings I assign to my experiences within particular intersubjective contexts. From this point of view, rather than being an obstacle to analytic functioning, listening to myself listening to the patient becomes a necessary and essential way of gathering, monitoring, exploring, and elaborating the data of experience.

The goal, to the extent there is one (it might be better to speak of the intention), is to realize and extend this resting state, to open a shared space for experience where intuition can be valued. Intuition is a tool for the clinician's mature use of the self, and it is likewise a vehicle for the patient's discovery of his own growing capacity for honesty and sincerity in exploring the truth of the impact of his own life experiences upon his developing identity.

Amy

I would now like to describe a bit of my work with a girl I will call Amy. I met Amy when she was four years old. She is the younger of two children. I will call her parents Sam and Nancy. Sam and Nancy received my name from a colleague who provided marital therapy. This person had heard a great deal about Amy because of the strain created by her early, complex medical issues and the impact of these traumatic realities upon the couple.

At the time of our first meeting, Amy was often waking at night in terror. Her parents described her as inconsolable during such episodes. They said she could not be soothed and that her crying sometimes lasted for forty-five minutes or until she became exhausted and would fall back to sleep.

Amy, they reported, was tenaciously controlling. Her parents described her as fixated on doing things in the same way. She insisted that she have the same items, like favorite clothes, toys, or foods. When routines were varied Amy "melted down." I recommended that

Amy begin analysis, with sessions four times a week, and they agreed to give it a try.

Rather quickly Amy began to show me more and more of the violence of her internal world. Though I cannot describe the many varied and complex themes that emerged in this child's complicated five-and-a-half-year analysis, I want to try to give at least a flavor of our experience.

In the early phases of our work, Amy played out a scenario in which a powerful figure whom she named "the Castle Man" captured and tortured a baby doll simply named "the baby." Amy often "became" the Castle Man, and it was surprising and eerie to feel how much power to intimidate this little girl had when she spoke through this character.

Amy would instruct me to make the doll "cry like a baby." At such times her voice was dripping with contempt. I acted out the parts assigned to me which, as time passed, began to make a story about a captive, unprotected, terrified baby. Session after session the baby suffered, but the Castle Man seemed never to tire of cruelly torturing her.

Amy's play felt very concrete. There was little sense of give and take between us and little sense that it was pretend. I felt it important to pay very close attention to my own feelings. As time went by, I began to observe and name to myself sensations of fear, helplessness, frustration, aggravation, anger, bewilderment, uncertainty, confusion, and hopelessness.

When Amy said, in her Castle Man voice, "Make the baby talk," I explored giving voice to imagined baby experiences. "Why is this happening to me?" I would make the baby wonder. "What have I done wrong?" "I'm so scared." "Won't someone please try to help me?" Initially this sort of play had an interesting effect. It seemed to increase the violence of the Castle Man. I became worried about stimulating this cruelty as if I were somehow affirming it, rather than trying to contain and comprehend it.

At the same time, however, my intuition was that something was evolving in this play. It was not simply repetition. Though it felt traumatizing *to me*, our meetings seemed to be an important outlet for Amy, who, her parents reported, was calming at home, sleeping through the night, but still fixated upon having things her way as far as her routines went.

I felt that I was gradually learning from experience something about an internal emotional atmosphere that caused Amy's night terrors and meltdowns. I saw myself as imaginatively visiting Amy's internal world. I was learning how to participate in it rather than just interpreting it from a distance. I felt I had to get to know her experience through my participation in the play in order to understand it more deeply and to find words for our experiences. I paid careful attention to the atmosphere that was evoked in the sessions.

Gradually Amy took more interest in the experience of the baby. The session that I want to describe came midway into our work. The play had evolved to include an entire family of figures struggling to make a life for themselves in a kingdom adjoining the realm of the Castle Man. It appeared to me that the Castle Man was no longer as powerful or as compelling a figure, and that Amy was hesitantly becoming curious to know something about the father and mother figures living in the new kingdom.

Amy began to ask things like "What are they thinking?" I would ask her to tell me what she thought. Sometimes she would give voice to the figures, but other times she would say "You make them talk." I did my best to imagine words for the parent figures. I imagined trying to put into words things I thought her own parents might have said or had not been able to say.

I would talk about how the mother and father were concerned to protect the baby from the Castle Man. I talked about feelings of love and confusion, of fear and of frustration. Amy would listen carefully. Sometimes she would say "keep talking" or "say more." Sometimes she would gaze intensely into my eyes as if I were speaking a foreign language and she were listening to the music of my voice.

Repeatedly the Castle Man would intrude on these periods of connection, either in the same session or on the following day. I would describe the sequences of response or reply, starting as best I could with the feeling of what was happening between us. I had the sense that we had to repeatedly live through things together and that it was this being with each other under all kinds of conditions and finding ways to describe the experiences that was gradually starting to make a difference to Amy in a deep way.

Amy began to tell me what the mother or father or baby might be thinking. She would give them ideas about how they might protect themselves from the Castle Man. For example, the family built shields and power plants to protect themselves. An elaborate system of barriers and filters was explored in her play.

It seemed to me that Amy always lived at least partially in the realm of the Castle Man wherever she was. This impression took on a certain organizing power for me. One day, when it felt right, I interpreted this to her. I can't remember exactly what I said, but I was interpreting how she lived close to and always under the influence of the Castle Man. She confirmed this to me, saying that yes, she always "listened to the Castle Man." She said he often talked to her throughout the day and that she also dreamt about him. This felt like an awesome moment to me. Finally Amy and I were talking together about her relationship to the Castle Man. She was emerging from living within his shadow, and I could imagine a day when she would be able to appreciate that the Castle Man was a part of herself, a personification, an attitude generated, I believed, from her own traumatic but at the same time life-saving medical experiences.

Amy and I began to speak very directly to each other about her relationship to the Castle Man. I think this became possible because of the background sense of trust and understanding that had been built up between us. Such moments of meeting are hard to describe. It was during this period of time that the session I want to report occurred.

Amy entered the session in a state of absolute emotional storm. Her father had carried her to the door, and she was screaming and crying. Her father explained that she had woken up saying she didn't want to go to Jeffrey's. He had, amazingly, brought her anyway, which I think took a lot of guts.

Amy screamed "Daddy don't leave me here, don't go, don't go." She clung to his legs. He gently pushed her into my room and shut the door. Amy looked at me with what I suppose was abject disbelief. She turned back to the door and with her nose right up against it screamed "Daddy, Daddy, please come back. Please. Please." Then she threw herself on my couch and began to scream "I want to go home." She cried for a very long time. I don't remember what I said. I tried to speak several times but she could not take in anything, or whatever I did say felt wrong to her and she began screaming again—piercing, full-body screams.

I sat down on the floor and began to wonder what this all might mean. I tried to listen to myself listening to Amy screaming. The first thing I felt was that I had to calm her down, I had to make her stop crying. But then I began to relax a little bit. I thought, I must tolerate her crying, be present to her crying, make space for her crying inside of me. Could I listen to the sound of her crying and screaming and pay attention to my own feelings about the impact? I felt I needed to let her crying wash over me and fill up the room.

I say this without wanting to sound sentimental. After a few minutes I almost began to hear a kind of music in Amy's crying. It was as if there were a very broken melody, albeit a harsh one, buried within the sound and rhythm of her crying. This strange broken melody included her gasping for air, her sniffling and choking, but mostly was the ebb and flow of the tones of her crying itself.

I had many experiences during the next several minutes. I felt I must have somehow become the Castle Man and that Amy now felt herself to be the baby. Then I had a strange thought, or a thought that felt strange to me. I imagined Amy was realizing that there was no real Castle Man and she was missing him. Then I felt that she might be finding herself, that she existed in a real family, with a real mother, a real father, a real brother, a real dog. I thought, I must be very real to her right now in a way that I have never been before. I thought, she is real to me in a way that seems new. I imagined she might be terribly frightened of something happening to one or both of us. I imagined she was feeling some new sense of self in all its utter complexity and intensity that there was no way a six-year-old could describe to herself or to anyone else. I imagined what it must have been like for her to be afraid of dying, because in reality, as a baby, she might have died several times as a result of her medical condition. I said all this, or something like it, to Amy *in my mind*.

Amy had covered herself with the blanket on the couch. Her crying had subsided. I wondered what to say and thought that it was okay to remain silent for a little bit longer. I had the vivid sensation-fantasy that Amy was my own child and that I was rocking her to sleep in my lap. In fact I was across the room sitting on the floor.

Finally I noticed Amy stirring under the blanket. I put this into words saying something like "I see you beginning to move beneath the blanket." There was no reply verbally. But Amy stuck one tiny finger out from beneath the blanket. I said, "I think you are checking to see if I am still here. Maybe you are trying to decide if you are ready to come out now." She put her whole hand out as if signaling me to take it. I didn't move. She then lifted the blanket and peeked out at me with one eye. I said, "I see you." She then came out from under the blanket and came and sat by me and put her head on my knee. My sense was that Amy was acknowledging something profound shared between us, not just in this session but also over the whole course of our work thus far. I knew she couldn't hear the thoughts I had said to her in my mind, but in some way I felt and imagined that she had "heard" me and that it had made a difference. I said to her something like "You have come a very long way back to find this calm and quiet place right now." Then she pretended to go to sleep. We sat in silence like this for the remainder of the session. At last I told her that it was time for our session to end and for me to let her father in.

Concluding Thoughts

Many things occurred to me as I listened to myself listening to Amy. I experienced a variety of internal replies that I allowed myself to speak to myself as I tracked the moment-to-moment experience of being with her. I tried to allow myself to register the impact of her crying within me. Before rushing to stop it or to interpret its meaning, I had to allow her crying to penetrate me. I needed to register the experience of listening to myself listening to her. What arises, then, in such an experience, is the unique product of that moment-to-moment encounter with another embodied subject. The fruit of such an encounter is a transformation in the quality of experience and also of the language used to represent that experience.

Words, when I can finally find them—or, to be more precise, when they finally find me—come, as it were, from the inside out. In such moments, I might have the courage to allow myself to be spoken through.

I believe, too, that moments of this kind reveal the important place of the intersubjective third (Ogden) or the bi-personal field (Ferro). Interpretations in such instances are not the product of my conscious reflection or even unconscious receptiveness alone. Instead, they are, at best, descriptions of what the Irish poet Seamus Heaney calls "the music of what happens."

Listening to yourself listening to another involves mindfulness and reverie. The quality of this attention is focused on the sensory level of experience. I am open to the images of visual, auditory, tactile, motor, and memory traces that arise while listening to the other. These sensation-images may become proto-scenes. Such scenes may generate a certain emotional atmosphere within me and between me and my patient. These scenes may be discernibly peopled with part-object, whole-object, and other emerging characters. Gradually or rapidly, as I "watch" the scenes and characters unfold in my mind's eye, I recognize proto-narrative patterns that organize incipient experience. Themes emerge that can be tentatively related to the here-and-now experience as it is unfolding.

The capacity for reverie sponsors the development of a deepening and evolving analytic process. This process is not governed by the analyst alone but is shared with the patient. Listening to myself listening to my patient expands the field of observation that sponsors the analytic process. My hope is that the patient also risks developing the capacity for self-observation within the context of a containing relationship. As this experience unfolds, the process of free association opens widely, and a willingness to tolerate the surprises that emerge in analytic space furthers the adventure of learning from experience.

References

Acquarone, S., and J. Raphael-Leff. (2007). *Signs of Autism in Infants: Recognition and Early Intervention*. London: Routledge.

Alvarez, A. (1992). *Live Company*. London: Routledge.

Alvarez, A., and P. Furgiuele. (1997). "Speculations on Components in the Infant's Sense of Agency: The Sense of Abundance and the Capacity to Think in Parenthesis." In S. Reid, ed., *Developments in Infant Observation: The Tavistock Model*, 123–39. London: Routledge.

Alvarez, A., and S. Reid. (1999). *Autism and Personality: Findings from the Tavistock Autism Workshop*. London: Routledge.

Beebe, B., and F. Lachmann. (2002). *Infant Research and Adult Treatment: Co-constructing Interactions*. Hillsdale, NJ: The Analytic Press.

Bion, W. R. (1957). "On Arrogance." In *Second Thoughts*, 86–92. London: Karnac, 1984.

———. (1959). "Attacks on Linking." In *Second Thoughts*, 93–109. London: Karnac, 1984.

———. (1961). *Experiences in Groups*. London: Tavistock Publications.

———. (1962a). "A Theory of Thinking." In *Second Thoughts*, 110–19. London: Karnac, 1984.

———. (1962b). *Learning from Experience*. London: Heinemann.

———. (1970). *Attention and Interpretation*. London: Tavistock Publications.

———. (1977). *Seven Servants: Four Works by W. R. Bion*. New York: Jason Aronson.

———. (1984). *Second Thoughts: Selected Papers on Psycho-Analysis*. London: Karnac, 1984. First publication: London: Heinemann, 1967.

———. (1985). *The Long Weekend: Part of a Life and All My Sins Remembered*. Perthshire: Clunie Press.

———. (2005). *The Italian Seminars*, P. Slotkin translator. London: Karnac.

Bollas, C. (1999). "Figures and Their Functions." In *The Mystery of Things*, 30–39. London: Routledge.

Boris, H. (1993). *Passions of the Mind: Unheard Melodies, A Third Principle of Mental Functioning*. New York: New York University Press.

Bronstein, C. (2001). *Kleinian Theory: A Contemporary Perspective*. London: Whurr; New York: Wiley.

Buckingham, L. (2002). "The Hazards of Curiosity: A Kleinian Perspective on Learning." In D. Barford, ed., *The Ship of Thought: Essays on Psychoanalysis and Learning*, 106–135. London: Karnac.

Caper, R. (1988). *Immaterial Facts: Freud's Discovery of Psychic Reality and Klein's Development of His Work*. Northvale, NJ: Jason Aronson.

Chiesa, M. (2001). "Envy and Gratitude." In C. Bronstein, ed., *Kleinian Theory: A Contemporary Perspective*, 93–107. London: Bruner Routledge.

Chodron, P. (1997). *When Things Fall Apart: Heart Advice for Difficult Times*. Boston: Shambhala.

Coltart, N. (1992). *Slouching Towards Bethlehem*. New York: Guilford.

Edwards, J. (2001). *Being Alive: Building on the Work of Anne Alvarez*. London: Brunner Routledge.

Eigen, M. (1986). *The Psychotic Core*. Northvale, NJ: Jason Aronson. London: Karnac Books, 2004.

———. (1992). *Coming through the Whirlwind*. Wilmette, IL: Chiron.

———. (1993). *The Electrified Tightrope*. Northvale, NJ: Jason Aronson. London: Karnac Books, 2004.

———. (1995). *Reshaping the Self: Reflections on Renewal through Therapy*. Madison, CT: Psychosocial Press.

———. (1996). *Psychic Deadness*. Northvale, NJ: Jason Aronson. London: Karnac Books, 2004.

Ferro, A. (1999). *The Bi-personal Field: Experiences in Child Analysis*. London: Routledge. New Library of Psychoanalysis 38.

Freud, S. (1911). "Formulations on the Two Principles of Mental Functioning." In E. Jones and J. Strachey, eds., *Collected Papers*, IV: 13–21. New York: Basic Books, 1959.

———. (1912). "Recommendations to Physicians on the Psycho-Analytic Method of Treatment." In E. Jones and J. Strachey, eds., *Collected Papers*, II: 323–33. New York: Basic Books.

Ginsburg, A. (1959). "Song." In *Howl and Other Poems*, 50–53. San Francisco: City Lights.

Gooch, J. (2002). "The Primitive Somatopsychic Roots of Gender Formation and Intimacy: Sensuality, Symbolism, and Passion in the Development of Mind." In S. Alhanati, ed., *Primitive Mental States. Volume II: Psychobiological and Psychoanalytic Perspectives on Early Trauma and Personality Development*, 159–173. London: Karnac.

Greenberg, M., and J. Snell. (1997). "Brain Development and Emotional Development: The Role of Teaching in Organizing the Frontal Lobe." In P. Salovey and D. J. Sluyter, eds., *Emotional Development and Emotional Intelligence: Educational Implications*, 93–111. New York: Basic Books.

Grotstein, J. S. (1980) "A Proposed Revision of the Psychoanalytic Concept of Primitive Mental States. Part I. Introduction to a Newer Psychoanalytic Metapsychology." *Contemporary Psychoanalysis* 16: 479–546.

———. (2000) *Who Is the Dreamer Who Dreams the Dream? A Study of Psychic Presences*. Hillsdale, NJ: The Analytic Press.

Hahn, T. N. (1998). *The Heart of Buddha's Teachings: Transforming Suffering into Peace, Joy, and Liberation*. New York: Broadway Books.

Harris-Williams, M., ed. (2005). *The Vale of Soulmaking*. London: Karnac.

Houzel, D., and M. Rhode. (2005). *Invisible Boundaries*. London: Karnac.

Huxley, A. (1929). "The Critic in the Crib." In R. Baker and J. Sexton, eds., *Aldous Huxley: Complete Essays, Volume III: 1930–1935*, 10–13. Chicago: Ivan R. Dee, 2001.

Jabès, E. (1987). *The Book of Questions*. Middletown, CT: Wesleyan University Press.

James, W. (1890). *Principles of Psychology*. Vol. 1. New York: Henry Holt and Company.

Lampen, J. (1987). *Mending Hurt: Swarthmore Lecture*. London: Quaker Home Services.

Levine, S. (1989). *A Gradual Awakening*. New York: Anchor/Doubleday.

Lopez-Corvo, R. E. (2003). *The Dictionary of the Work of W. R. Bion*. London: Karnac.

———. (2006). *Wild Thoughts Searching for a Thinker*. London: Karnac.

Meltzer, D. (1967). *The Psycho-Analytical Process*. Perthshire: Clunie Press.

————. (1975). *Explorations in Autism: A Psycho-Analytical Study.* Strath Tay, Perthshire: Clunie Press.

————. (1983). *Dream-Life: A Re-examination of the Psycho-analytic Theory and Technique.* Perthshire: Clunie Press, for the Roland Harris Trust, 1984.

————. (1988). "Concerning the Stupidity of Evil." In A. Hahn, ed., *Sincerity and Other Works: Collected Papers of Donald Meltzer,* 561–63. London: Karnac, 1994.

————. (1992). *The Claustrum: An Investigation of Claustrophobic Phenomena.* Perthshire: Clunie Press.

————. (2005). "Creativity and Countertransference." In M. Harris-Williams, M., ed., *The Vale of Soulmaking,* 175–182. London: Karnac.

Mitrani, J. (1996). *A Framework for the Imaginary: Clinical Explorations in Primitive Mental States.* Northvale, NJ: Jason Aronson.

Mitrani, J., and T. Mitrani. (1997). *Encounters with Autistic States: Memorial Tribute to Frances Tustin.* Northvale: Jason Aronson.

Nairn, R. (1999). *Diamond Mind: A Psychology of Meditation.* Boston: Shambhala.

Ogden, T. H. (1999). "The Analytic Third: An Overview." *fort da* 5 (1), an online publication of the Northern California Society for Psychoanalytic Psychology; also available at www.therapyvlado.com/index. php?id=4&article=1695.

Pally, R. (2000). *The Mind-Brain Relationship.* London: Karnac.

Rhode, M., and T. Klauber. (2004). *The Many Faces of Asperger's Syndrome.* London: Karnac.

Sandler, P. (2005). *The Language of Bion: A Dictionary of Concepts.* London: Karnac.

Snyder, G. (1996). Interview with Eliot Weinberger. In George Plimpton, ed., *Beat Writers at Work / Paris Review,* 275–98. London: Harvill Press, 1999.

Stern, D., and L. Sander, J. Nahum, A. Harrison, N. Bruschweiler-Stern, N. and E. Tronik. (1998). "Non-Interpretative Mechanisms in Psychoanalytic Therapy: The 'Something More' than Interpretation." *International Journal of Psychoanalysis* 79: 903–21.

Symington, J. (1985). "The Survival Function of Primitive Omnipotence." *International Journal of Psychoanalysis* 66: 481–87.

Tremelloni, L. (2005). *Arctic Spring.* London: Karnac.

Tustin, F. (1986). *Autistic Barriers in Neurotic Patients.* New Haven, CT: Yale University Press.

―――. (1992). *Autistic States in Children.* London: Routledge.

Winnicott, D. (1959). "Review of Envy and Gratitude." In C. Winnicott, R. Shepherd, and M. Davis, eds., *Psychoanalytic Explorations,* 443–46. Cambridge, MA: Harvard University Press, 1989.

―――. (1990). *Playing and Reality.* London: Routledge.

Young, S. (1997). *The Science of Enlightenment.* Boulder: Sounds True Audio.

Made in the USA
San Bernardino, CA
02 September 2015